Understanding the
Political Spirit: Philosophical
Investigations from
Socrates to Nietzsche

Contributors

CATHERINE H. ZUCKERT is Professor of Political Science at Carleton College in Northfield, Minnesota. She has published articles on Aristotle, Tocqueville, Nietzsche, and various classic American novelists.

ARLENE W. SAXONHOUSE is Professor of Political Science at the University of Michigan, Ann Arbor. In addition to several articles on ancient Greek literature and philosophy, she has written a book on *Women in the History of Political Thought: Ancient Greece to Machiavelli*.

MARY P. NICHOLS is the Visiting Scholar for Honors Education at the University of Delaware. Her writings include *Socrates and the Political Community: An Ancient Debate*, as well as articles on Rousseau and Shakespeare.

ANN P. CHARNEY is Associate Professor of Political Science at Rosary College, River Forest, Illinois. She is currently editing a collection of essays on Aristotle's *Politics*.

HARVEY C. MANSFIELD, JR., is Professor of Government at Harvard University. His books include *Statesmanship and Party Government, The Spirit of Liberalism*, and *Machiavelli's New Modes and Orders*.

DAVID LOWENTHAL is Professor of Political Science at Boston College. He has edited and translated Montesquieu's *Considerations on the Causes of the Greatness of the Romans and Their Decline*.

TIMOTHY FULLER is Professor of Political Science at Colorado College. He edits the *International Hobbes Association Newsletter* and has published on liberalism, authority, and the nature of modern political philosophy.

NATHAN TARCOV is Associate Professor of Political Science and in the College at the University of Chicago. He is author of *Locke's Education for Liberty*.

MICHAEL GILLESPIE is Associate Professor of Political Science at Duke University and author of *Hegel, Heidegger, and the Ground of History*.

WERNER DANNHAUSER is Professor of Government at Cornell University and author of *Nietzsche's View of Socrates*.

Edited by
Catherine H. Zuckert

Understanding the Political Spirit: Philosophical Investigations from Socrates to Nietzsche

Yale University Press
New Haven and London

Designed by Jo Aerne and set in Bembo
type with Janson display by Rainsford
Type, Ridgefield, Connecticut.
Printed in the United States of America
by Book Crafters, Inc., Chelsea,
Michigan.

Library of Congress Cataloging-in-
Publication Data
Understanding the political spirit.
Based on papers presented at a confer-
ence "On the role of spiritedness in pol-
itics" which was sponsored by the
National Endowment for the Humani-
ties. 1. Political science—Philosophy—
Congresses. 2. Political psychology—
Congresses. I. Zuckert, Catherine H.,
1942– . II. National Endowment for the
Humanities.
JA74.U53 1988 320'.01 87–10231
ISBN 0–300–03899–2 (alk. paper)

The paper in this book meets the guidelines for permanence and durability of the
Committee on Production Guidelines
for Book Longevity of the Council on
Library Resources.

10 9 8 7 6 5 4 3 2 1

To Joseph Cropsey

Whose thought has here quickened thought,
Whose craftsmanship has inspired emulation,
Whose strength and honor have elicited admiration,
And whose friendship and care
have provoked gratitude and love.
From his friends and students.

M. Z.

Contents

Acknowledgments

We would like to take this opportunity to thank several institutions and individuals who have helped us complete this book. First, we thank Michael Zuckert, who played a decisive role in selecting the topic for this book and the authors of the particular chapters. Second, we acknowledge our debt to the National Endowment for the Humanities for sponsoring a conference, "On the Role of Spiritedness in Politics," at which most of the chapters in this book were initially delivered and critiqued. We would also like to thank the Olin Center at the University of Chicago for hosting the conference. We are particularly grateful to Erica Aronson and Gary Coleman for their assistance in organizing and conducting that meeting. Finally, our thanks to Hendrika Umbanhowar for her care and patience in typing and retyping the manuscript.

CATHERINE
H. ZUCKERT

I

On the Role of
Spiritedness in Politics

Among the many analyses of our politically troubled times,
Joseph Cropsey's treatment of "The United States as Regime"
stands out for its rich interweaving of theoretical and practical
considerations, as well as for the novelty and suggestiveness of
its concluding prescription. The "United States is a microcosm
of modernity, repeating in its regime, on the level of popular
consciousness, the major noetic events of the modern world"
(p. 13).[1] Not only is this nation explicitly based on principles
derived from classic modern political philosophers like Thomas
Hobbes and John Locke, but the limitations these liberal principles put on the powers of government, particularly with respect
to restrictions of the freedom of speech, also insure that the
criticisms made of these principles will be publicly propounded.
As Cropsey says, "The United States is an arena in which modernity is working itself out. The founding documents are the
premise of a gigantic argument, subsequent propositions in
which are the decayed or decaying moments of modern thought,
superimposed on relics of antiquity" (p. 7).

Modern political principles generate their own critique,
Cropsey suggests, because modernity itself is divided into
"tougher" and "softer" branches.

> While the transition from Machiavelli to Hobbes
> might appear to be a simple evolution . . . , it in fact
> includes a development that should not be over-
> looked. Machiavelli can be understood as teaching a
> lesson intended to harden and inspirit men. Hobbes,

> teaching life, liberty, and the pursuit of happiness,
> prepared what came to be known as the bourgeoisi-
> fication of life. . . . From its inception, modernity has
> exhibited two moral meanings or tendencies, one in-
> spiriting, reminding man of his earth-bound solitude
> and presenting the world as an opportunity for great-
> ness of some description, the other pointing toward
> survival, security, and freedom to cultivate the pri-
> vate and privately-felt predilections. . . . The tension
> between the two dispositions persists throughout the
> modern age. (Pp. 6–7)

In America, the presence of the two branches of modernity has
meant that the dominant bourgeois moral tendency has repeatedly been criticized as ignoble, inauthentic, repressive, egoistic,
materialistic, and unduly narrow (or ethnocentric) on socialist,
existential, psychological, religious, and even scientific grounds.
In each case the critique draws from the more stringent branch
of modern thought, but the effect has not been to elevate the
goals of the regime or to make American morals more austere
so much as to justify further self-indulgence. The waves of criticism create an even greater need to remind human beings of
their higher aspirations. "Our prospects in our third century,"
Cropsey concludes, "appear to depend on the possibility that
our moral resources will incline to fortify themselves at the spirited wells of modernity."

In order to understand Cropsey's analysis of American self-
dissatisfaction, much less to respond to it, we need to understand
what he means by these "spirited wells." *Spiritedness* is no longer
a common term in popular political parlance. If we turn to Plato's
Republic, however, we see that Socrates identified *thymos*, or
spiritedness, as the psychic origin of distinctively political action.
Has our understanding of the psychological foundations of political life changed so fundamentally that we no longer recognize
the existence of that thing the ancients called spiritedness?[2] Are
we then missing a fundamental aspect of our existence, both as
individuals and in communities? Or is it simply that we are

talking about the same thing, but in different terms? This volume is devoted to answering these questions.

Spiritedness: The Phenomenon

In order to understand what is meant by spiritedness, it is useful to look at the early books of the *Republic*. Here Plato gives his fullest and most systematic account of the phenomenon in the process of drawing his famous analogy between the parts and order of the city and the parts and order of the soul. As the city is divided into money-making, auxiliary, and guardian classes, Socrates argues, so the individual soul contains a desiring, a spirited, and a calculating or reasoning part. In both city and person, the spirited part serves to maintain order and unity by checking the divisive effects of unjust desires. As the city needs spirited warriors to defend it from external aggression, so individual rulers must be taught to use the spirited part of their soul to control their potentially tyrannous inclinations. The source of protection from both foreign domination and internal oppression, spiritedness appears to constitute the psychological root of political independence. It thus seems strange that the phenomenon has almost fallen out of sight in modern times.

One reason we have lost sight of the phenomenon of spiritedness is that we tend to take an economizing view of politics. Americans have been taught that human beings are endowed by their creator with inalienable rights to life, liberty, and the pursuit of happiness, and that governments are instituted to secure these rights. Political order thus appears to constitute the means best calculated to help us realize our private desires. Government at least establishes the conditions under which these desires (or preferences) can be achieved. In contrast to this view, Socrates suggests that if human beings were content to live with what they need to preserve themselves and the species, they could live in peace and amity with no political order whatsoever. If each does what he or she does best by nature and trades with others, all can meet their needs and still live as equals without any division into rulers and ruled. Socrates argues, in contrast to Marx's later theory, that it is not the division of labor in itself that causes conflict and oppression. It is rather the desire to have more than they need and to be recognized as better that leads human beings to attack the lands and lives of other human beings.

According to Socrates, then, political order does not emerge directly from the requirements of self-preservation but indirectly from the need people experience to defend their lives, lands, and liberty from the dominating designs of others. Political order does not arise directly from one's own desires or the means best calculated to realize those desires but rather in reaction to the excessive desires of others. The psychological source of political order is not to be found in either the desires or reason, therefore, but in the phenomenon Socrates calls spiritedness.

In its spirited origins, we find some of the reasons political life is so difficult to understand. People would not fight to defend their own lives, lands, and liberties, if they were not extremely attached to them. Spiritedness is thus rooted in love of one's own; yet we observe that in fighting to defend them, the warrior risks the very life, liberty, and property he is presumably struggling to preserve. There is something potentially contradictory about a spirited defense of one's own except in the most dire circumstances, that is, in the instance of an immediate, non-avoidable attack in which one will certainly lose his life if he does not resist. The suspicion that human spiritedness is not altogether reasonable grows when we see, as in the case of Achilles, that spiritedness manifests itself most commonly as rage.

As rage, spiritedness reveals itself to be a reaction to the frustration of desire.[3] As Socrates observes, however, mature human beings do not react with equal anger to all disappointment or affliction.

> The nobler [a man] is, won't he be less capable of anger at suffering hunger, cold or anything else of the sort inflicted on him by one whom he supposes does so justly . . . ? [But] when a man believes he's

being done injustice? Doesn't his spirit in this case
boil and become harsh and form an alliance for battle
with what seems just; and, even if it suffers in hunger,
cold and everything of the sort, doesn't it stand firm
and conquer, and not cease from its noble efforts
before it has succeeded, or death intervenes . . . ? (*Republic* 440c–d)

In its particular attachment to justice, spiritedness again reveals
its political character. And it is through this attachment to justice
that Socrates attempts to show that spiritedness can be used to
unite the community internally as well as externally.

Once a community has defenders, Socrates recognizes, a
political order emerges de facto, because it is clear that the armed
citizens will command—rule—their unarmed fellows.[4] Thus,
once political order emerges, the problem of checking the unjust
desires becomes even more pressing internally than it was externally. For how are the armed rulers to be prevented from
using their power to extract more than they need from their
weaker subjects? The guardians can check the unjust desires of
the farmers and mechanics by making and enforcing laws, for
example, of fair trade. But who is to police the policemen?

Socrates introduces his tripartite analysis of the human psyche in the *Republic* to show that it is possible to avoid political
oppression by forming the souls of the ruling class so that they
will control themselves. As the unjust desires of foreign invaders
can be checked by spirited warriors, if they are properly trained,
so the potentially tyrannous desires of individual rulers can be
controlled by the spirited part of their souls, if they are properly
educated.

Most of us have had the experience of wanting something,
yet having something else inside us check that inclination. That
which checks the desires internally is our spiritedness, Socrates
explains. By admonishing us internally, it joins with our reason
to enforce publicly accepted standards of right behavior against
our desires.

Viewed internally and individually, spiritedness looks very
much like what we have come to call conscience. And as Socrates

indicates through the example of Leontius, spiritedness is equally
(in)effective.[5] Human beings may castigate themselves for doing
wrong, but when the desire proves strong enough, like Leontius
they act contrary to their inner voice or command. Some desires
or aversions are too powerful to be eradicated or controlled
simply through persuasion or training. In order to prevent the
guardians from using their power to extract more goods and
services than they need from the farmers and mechanics, their
education must be supplemented by laws that deprive them of
anything of their own—family, dwelling, property, or privacy.
The guardians must watch other guardians as well as themselves.
It is, unfortunately, easier to enforce legal restrictions on others
than to restrain oneself.

Critics since Aristotle have observed, however, that the
communistic institutions Socrates proposes in the *Republic* will
not work.[6] Bereft of any particular stake in the community, the
guardians have no particular reason to serve it. Separated from
love of one's own, spiritedness does not operate; and its roots
in man's attachment to his own existence make spiritedness less
than perfectly reasonable or public-spirited. A man may risk his
life to defend his homeland, but if he survives, he will claim his
"just" reward. The thought that the rulers ought to receive
more—honor or money or freedom or power—to compensate
them for their public service is the cause of the degeneration of
regimes Socrates portrays in Book VIII of the *Republic*. As Aristotle observes in the *Politics*, all groups contribute something
to the polity as a whole and all tend to value their own contri-
butions more than other groups do. Continuing deliberation and
conflict about the just distribution of rewards are thus endemic
to all political orders.

By constructing a model of a regime in which rulers receive
nothing but what they need to survive, Socrates does show that
exercising political power has no intrinsic advantage or attraction. With no external rewards, in the *Republic* the guardians
have to be forced to serve. Human beings do not willingly sacrifice their own desires to the interests of others. Those who
seek political office obviously do not seek it for its own sake,
but as a means of satisfying other, more self-rewarding wants.

Just men enter politics only when they feel obliged to pay back the city for their education or to protect themselves and their loved ones from the unjust designs of others. To do either they must be extremely spirited. To Socrates, spiritedness is both the origin and the motive force of political life.

By comparing the psychological foundations of the regime in the *Republic* with more modern accounts, we discover a second reason the concept has fallen into disuse. Where Socrates speaks of a soul divided into desire, spiritedness, and reason, post-Christian thinkers describe the human psyche in terms of passion, will, and mind. Like spiritedness, will can be combined with or subordinated to either reason, as in Augustine's rational will and Rousseau's general will, or passion, as in Hobbes and Locke and Nietzsche's will to power. And like spiritedness, will is often conceived as the psychological foundation of human self-determination or independence (the free will). Unlike spiritedness, however, will is not particularly associated with righteous indignation or justice. Will appears to be more individualistic, associated more with choice than with punishment, and hence less political than spiritedness.

Have we then lost a sense of the true psychological foundations of politics by shifting our focus from spiritedness to will? Are we missing something essential by no longer understanding political life primarily as a means of resisting injustice but rather conceiving it largely as a means of realizing our desires? Or is understanding politics basically in terms of liberty both simpler and more effective? Although spiritedness and love of liberty have much in common, we shall see in the following chapters that there are important differences.

The Ancient Understanding of the
Need to Tame Spiritedness

For Plato and Aristotle, Achilles represents the embodiment of spiritedness, or thymos. In chapter 2, Arlene Saxonhouse thus examines "*Thymos*, Justice, and Moderation of Anger in the Story of Achilles."

In Achilles, spiritedness first appears to be attached to a concern for honor. When Agamemnon takes his prize and so dishonors him, Achilles angrily withdraws from battle. Achilles is not merely reacting to a personal slight, however; as Saxonhouse points out, he is objecting to Agamemnon's undermining the accepted system of distribution of rewards whereby warriors are entitled to at least some of the spoils they take in battle.

Spiritedness is associated with a sense of injustice. And as Achilles sits on the sidelines and meditates on his future course of action, his sense of injustice grows. He knows that even great warriors are only mortal. If he were to lose his life in battle, he could never enjoy the honor or goods given him for his service. The rational course of action, he concludes, is to return home and live in obscurity. There is no reward that can compensate a man for risking his life.

There may not be any reward for virtue, but there is the rage that leads a man to strike back at those who have harmed him. Rather than go home, Achilles eventually returns to battle to avenge the death of his friend Patroclus. By doing so, he explicitly accepts the loss of his own life as the price of revenge. In a world ruled by the Olympian gods, the only justice is what each man does himself. (As Achilles observes in Book XXIV of the *Iliad*, there are three jars before Zeus's door from which individual human fates are drawn, apparently at random.) Unfortunately, Achilles discovers for a second time, in the absence of cosmic or divine support, all human systems of exchange prove to be imperfect. Nothing he can do to Hector's body can compensate for, or reconcile Achilles to, the loss of his friend. Achilles' grief and anger end, therefore, only when the gods command it. He can find no satisfaction by or in himself. Although he declares a truce to enable Priam to bury Hector, according to custom, we know that Achilles will reenter the battle in which both he and Troy will be destroyed.

To harness human spiritedness in order to make it protective rather than destructive of human life, both Plato and Aristotle suggest, it is necessary to replace the Homeric picture of a constantly changing cosmos ruled by capricious gods with a philosophic understanding of the natural order. Perceiving the unalterable necessity of their death, human beings will no longer rage incessantly against their fate. They will instead dedicate their efforts to perpetuating their blood and name or fame by striving to preserve their people. For Plato and Aristotle philosophy becomes the means of curbing spiritedness.

Spiritedness is a necessary quality of human beings who would live free from the oppression of others, Socrates observes in the *Republic,* because it is man's thymos that enables him to defend himself by overcoming his fear of death. Rightly nurtured, the spirited part of man's nature becomes courageous. If the development of the spirited part is not balanced by the development of the softer, wisdom-loving part, the man is apt to become harsh and rigid. The problem is that these two parts of the psyche seem to be opposed, so that development of the one destroys the development of the other. If a man devotes himself entirely to poetry (the work of the muse) and philosophy, his spirit becomes weak. If he devotes himself entirely to improving his fighting ability through physical exercise, however, his love of learning soon becomes enfeebled; even his senses are not sharpened.

The educational scheme Socrates proposes in the *Republic* is intended to overcome the opposition between philosophy and spiritedness. As we see in Book III, this education is devoted primarily to repressing the expression of the deep emotion characteristic of Achilles. But, as Mary P. Nichols argues in chapter 3, this education has problematic results.

To prevent the guardians from becoming overly harsh and tyrannous, they must be exposed to poetry; but the poetry they are to hear is purged of all its softening elements. The god(s) of which they hear will not exhibit any human failings. The extraordinarily self-controlled heroes of the epic poems recited in Socrates' polity will not lament or laugh. Nor does Socrates think such an education will suffice. To prevent the guardians from preferring their own interests to the community, they must also be deprived of all property, privacy, and particular family relations. As Adeimantus observes, theirs is hardly an enviable life.

Philosophy can overcome man's spirited attachment to his own life and kin, Socrates suggests, by showing him the beauty of the eternal ideas. In light of these, mortal affairs appear to be ephemeral illusions. But, Nichols argues, philosophers who have perceived the eternal consequently have to be forced to pay attention to the temporal affairs of the polity in order to rule. Caring nothing for their fellow citizens, these philosophers would not appear to be good rulers. Ignoring their own mortality and apparently oblivious of the requirements of their own self-preservation, they also seem to lack the self-knowledge that Socrates states is the sole goal of his own endeavors.[7] Rather than taming spiritedness with philosophy, Nichols concludes the scheme Socrates proposes in the *Republic* subordinates philosophy to a spirited desire to be completely self-sufficient, independent, and invincible. Instead of seeking self-knowledge or continually questioning received opinion, as Socrates himself does, the guardians merely try to preserve the established order. They are not truly philosophic seekers of knowledge or wisdom. The opposition between spiritedness and philosophy appears to be as unbridgeable at the end of Socrates' discussion as it had at the beginning. The problem of how to make the human spirit reasonable and philosophy politically effective thus remains for Aristotle.

Like Plato, Aristotle begins his analysis of spiritedness with a critique of the Homeric heroes. Describing the first of the moral virtues in the *Nichomachean Ethics*, Ann Charney points out in chapter 4, Aristotle distinguishes true courage from several apparent forms, including political courage and spiritedness. Homer provides examples only of the apparent forms of courage, the search for honor and the spirited, irrational desire for revenge, because belief in the arbitrary, willful, vengeful Homeric gods does not lead men rationally to assess what is to be feared. On the contrary, believing that the course of events is a product not of a necessary, fundamentally unchanging cosmic order, but rather of the "will of Zeus," Homeric heroes like Hector hope against all reason that somehow the gods will save them—as the gods can, if they do in fact rule the world by whim.[8] In order to tame thymos and make it a source of political unity rather than competitive division, Aristotle suggests, belief in the Homeric gods must be replaced with a more rational understanding of both the cosmos and the source or nature of human honor.

Human beings can participate in the immortal only through philosophic contemplation of the cosmic order or procreation of future generations. If our descendants are to survive, they must have a polity for their defense. Civic order does require a certain kind of philosophic foundation, but in contrast to Plato, Aristotle does not argue that philosophers must become rulers. Once it becomes clear that it is the polity and not the gods who guarantee the glory of the guardian, Aristotle argues, the foundations exist for a kind of exchange between the surviving citizens and their defenders. The exchange of goods, services, or honors, however, does not constitute an adequate basis for a political community. Friendship is also necessary. A man does not give his life in defense of his community simply for the sake of honor but finally as a magnanimous gift or sacrifice to the people he loves, who acknowledge rather than pay back his service by remembering it. By depriving guardians of anything of their own, Aristotle argues in the *Politics* (1261b–1262b), Plato deprives them of anything to fight for. And by destroying the family, he destroys the social or ethnic ties that form the basis of civic unity.

According to the ancient understanding, then, political community does not originate merely in · the natural desire for self-preservation common to all animals. Animals do not form polities. Only human beings do; and when human beings unite to defend their lives and property from external aggressors, they unite not merely from need but from a feeling that they are being wronged. The spirited part of the human soul is especially attached to this sense of wrong—or, positively stated, right (*dike*)—and thus forms the psychic basis of political unity. But, Plato and Aristotle both teach, if spiritedness in a city's rulers is not checked, these rulers are apt to become harsh and oppressive. To prevent rulers from tyrannizing over their fellow citizens, these rulers must be educated. In the first place, the Homeric view of a universe governed by willful gods must be replaced by a more philosophic understanding of the natural order. Where Plato would also deprive rulers of all property and family to prevent them from unjustly preferring their own to others in the city, Aristotle seeks to enlist the rulers' desire for honor as well as their attachment to kin to induce them to serve the city rather than their own material self-interest. In both cases, however, the solution to the political problem requires the city to remain small. If it grows too large, the city will become too wealthy to maintain the Spartan conditions required for Plato's philosophic rulers. The social or ethnic ties upon which Aristotle relies will also become too diluted to be effective.

Unfortunately, small polities are usually vulnerable to attack by their larger neighbors, as the Greek *poleis* were, first by Macedonia and second by Rome. And viewed in light of Roman history, the ancient understanding seems to be self-defeating. To whatever extent a ruling class effectively defends the city from external aggression, it seems, it also undermines the conditions for maintaining a just domestic order. Adhering to an austere moral code, Roman armies not only successfully defended their city but eventually conquered the known world. As both Livy and Machiavelli point out, the wealth and the cosmopolitanism of the empire they conquered finally undermined the public spirit of the Roman people, and with it the republic. Modern political philosophers thus had reason to question the adequacy of the ancient understanding.

Machiavelli and the Modern Attempt
to Reinspirit Men

By conquering the world, Roman armies created conditions that facilitated the spread of Christianity. But, Machiavelli observed, adoption of the Christian faith made it impossible for his contemporaries to emulate Roman virtue. As a result, his countrymen had difficulty maintaining their political independence.

> Reflecting now as to whence it came that in ancient times the people were more devoted to liberty than in the present, I believe that it resulted from this, that men were stronger in those days, which I believe to be attributable to the difference of education, founded in the difference of their religion and ours. For, our religion teaches us . . . to attach less value to the honors and possessions of this world; whilst the Pagans, esteeming those things as the highest good, were more energetic and ferocious in their actions.[9]

By teaching people that "the meek shall inherit the earth," Machiavelli thought, Christianity had made decent men too gentle, unable to defend their lives and liberties effectively from those less restrained by principle. Ancient political philosophers sought to moderate citizens' spirited attachment to their own goods and honor by having them contemplate the transitoriness of all temporal things in contrast to unchanging ideas. Machiavelli tried to turn his readers' attention away from concern for their eternal salvation to securing their secular self-interest. His work is an example of the inspiriting tendency or meaning of modern political philosophy.

Like the ancient philosophers, Machiavelli argued that it was necessary to reeducate rulers in order to enable them effectively to serve the interests of the community as a whole. But the education he proposed in *The Prince* was very different from that propounded in either Plato's *Republic* or Aristotle's *Nichomachean Ethics*. Socrates argued that it was necessary to educate guardian-warriors in order to make them gentler, for example, while Machiavelli stressed the need to teach political leaders "how not to be good."[10] More fundamental, Socrates tried to overcome the divisions within most polities, particularly between the rich and the poor, by teaching his rulers to dedicate themselves entirely to the community. Machiavelli not only sought to show the prince how to pursue his own interest most successfully but also advised him to use the notables and the people to check each other's worst tendencies.[11]

The difference between ancient and modern forms of the education of rulers comes out most graphically in Socrates' and Machiavelli's respective treatments of execution. It is thus with a consideration of Machiavelli's teaching on execution that Harvey C. Mansfield, Jr., begins his analysis of "Machiavelli and the Modern Executive." The major example Socrates provides of the operation of spiritedness in the individual in the *Republic* is the anger Leontius feels at his own weakness when he cannot restrain himself from looking at the corpses of executed traitors. The corpses remind Leontius of both the terrors of death and the potential division within the city, two factors that Socrates' educational system is designed to hide. Rather than deny or repress either fear or self-interest, Machiavelli counsels the prince to use both in order to maintain civic order. Both Socrates and Machiavelli seek to use man's spirit to discipline his desires. Where Socrates' educational system emphasizes self-control, however, Machiavelli looks primarily to external checks or restraints.

Although Socrates and Machiavelli offer different prescriptions, they are responding to the same problem. Because human beings generally desire more than they need, they come into conflict with one another unless their desires are somehow restrained. This is the reason government is necessary to keep order at home and to defend one's land from aggression abroad. According to both Socrates and Machiavelli, the checks on the desires of most human beings are thus primarily external. Most people restrain their desires primarily for fear of the consequences. Like the ancients, Machiavelli sees that rulers may use their arms to oppress their fellow citizens rather than to defend them. But he argues that teaching these rulers to concern themselves about the eternal rather than the earthly will not prevent them from oppressing their fellow citizens so much as it will lead them to neglect their duty. The most effective way of securing nonoppressive rule is to change the basis of political power from arms to popular consent.

So long as political power is the preserve of a warrior class, Machiavelli explains, the prince will be caught between the conflicting interests and demands of the people and his army. Both because armed soldiers are stronger than unarmed subjects and because the army is full of potential competitors, the prince who bases his rule on an armed class will find it necessary to oppress his people in order to satisfy his army's fierce passions.[12] The prince should therefore attempt to replace his mercenary troops with a citizen army whenever possible, that is, he should disband or destroy any distinctly military class.[13] To get citizens to fight for their prince, however, the executive must convince the people that they act in their own interest. That is, he must persuade them that he is their man. The best way to do this is to have the people choose him.[14] Machiavelli's elective executive represents his alternative to the ancient model of the general-statesman.

Ancient republics honored their generals—and, Machiavelli points out, models of political virtue like Scipio, Achilles, and Cyrus all have been generals—less for the courage and intelligence they displayed in defending the city than for their demonstrated ability to conquer others and so to enhance public prosperity through the extension of empire. The problem was that like Caesar such generals threatened to conquer their fellow citizens as well. In his description of the German city-states, Machiavelli intimates that a defensive federation of small, free republics that encourage the development of the arts of trade among their citizens might provide more popular prosperity and security than the military exploits of the most famous generals of the past, if the people are trained and armed.[15] To give political power a popular basis may not necessarily make it less spirited. It can rather make spiritedness safer and yet give it freer range.

In Machiavelli, then, we see the two fundamental ways in which modern political philosophy departs from the ancient understanding of the need to check the spiritedness that lies at the root of all political rule. Rather than seek to tame spiritedness in members of a ruling class, modern political philosophers attempt to arouse it in the populace as a whole. Rather than seek to arouse their spiritedness through an appeal to justice, moreover, modern political philosophers attempt to incite citizens to defend their country out of love of liberty. The definition of the political problem remains the same in both ancient and modern thought—how to avoid oppression, both foreign and domestic.

Popularizing Spiritedness as
Love of Liberty

Spiritedness does not disappear in the modern liberal state, Timothy Fuller, David Lowenthal, and Nathan Tarcov all argue, but it is transformed. Attached less to the conquest of others than to the preservation of one's own life, liberty, and property, in the modern liberal state spiritedness becomes not only more widespread or popular but also apparently more decent. The question is whether the importance of the phenomenon, if not the phenomenon itself, becomes lost when spiritedness acquires this more domesticated liberal form.

According to both Hobbes and Locke, Lowenthal reminds us, war is the condition that prevails among men before they establish government, and the object of government is to establish domestic peace and justice, as well as to maintain enough strength to resist foreign enemies. Of war's several causes, according to Hobbes, one of the foremost is the love of glory and superiority most often found in aristocratic monarchies or republics. Hobbes seeks to extirpate the search for honor from politics and to found a peaceful, rational order on the more pervasive fear of violent death. Hobbes retains Machiavelli's (and Socrates') insight into the foundations of political order in fear. Unlike Machiavelli, however, Hobbes seeks to attach both this fear and the people's general desire for prosperity to the rule of law, rather than to rulers' desire for preeminence.

Taking issue with Cropsey's claim that Hobbes "prepared

what came to be known as the bourgeoisification of life," Fuller argues that Hobbes's attempt to stifle vainglory (or unchecked spiritedness) does not destroy the possibility of true nobility. Rather than seek to conquer others, men of honor in the post-Hobbesian world will seek to control themselves. The external manifestation of this self-rule is law-abidingness, through which noble men obey their reason rather than follow their passions. Like Socrates and Machiavelli, Fuller acknowledges, Hobbes saw that most human beings obey the law for fear of the consequences; but the fact that most men are law-abiding for craven reasons does not destroy the nobility of the rule of law for those who follow it freely, of their own will, and not for fear of external punishment.

Where Hobbes sought to make human beings less spirited and more law-abiding through a combination of fear and reason, Tarcov argues, Locke thought the love of dominion could best be counteracted by love of liberty. To be sure, in the *Two Treatises* Locke's argument that human beings have a right to kill others in order to protect their liberties depends upon his regarding liberty as "necessary to and closely joyned with a man's preservation."[16] Because in the *Two Treatises* Locke is primarily concerned with showing the rights and duties of human beings according to the law of nature, he emphasizes the formulation of the right to liberty in a rational calculation of the means requisite to self-preservation. Although the persuasive power of this argument depends upon an appeal to love of liberty, such an appeal remains marginal to the primary argument.

Locke makes both the psychological grounds and significance of his appeal to the love of liberty explicit in *Some Thoughts Concerning Education*. As in the *Two Treatises*, Locke is anxious to defend the "industrious and rational against the quarrelsome and ambitious" and to provide against "the Natural Vanity and Ambition of Men, too apt by it self to grow and encrease with Possession of any Power," including both "the Ambitious Insolence of Empire" and "the Pride, Ambition, and Turbulency of private Man."[17] But, Locke observes, the most effective way to arouse human beings against this ambition, in themselves as well as in others, is not to appeal to their fears, their desire for pleasure, or their calculations about the most efficient means of achieving their goals, so much as to the pride they take in appearing to be both free and rational.

Locke shows that the love of dominion his education is intended to counter and the love of liberty it is meant to arouse are two aspects of the same psychological phenomenon by calling them both pride. The natural desire to preserve oneself suggests, at bottom, a certain amount of self-love. Self-love becomes self-esteem when it is associated with rationality and freedom. Where Aristotle sought to domesticate the desire for preeminence and conquest by attaching it primarily to love of one's own (constraining the scope or space in which the desire for preeminence is to operate), Locke attempts to civilize the tyrannical desire for gaining mastery over others by transforming it into the civil desire to have one's rights recognized by others. If, as Tarcov argues, the liberality and courage that disdain slavery are the positive sides of the phenomenon understood by classical political philosophy as thymos or spiritedness, it again serves as the cement of civil society. The "desire to be treated as a rational creature and show one is free is social in a way that merely sensual desires are not. It points toward a recognition of the liberty and rationality of others as the conditions of their recognition of one's own." The way in which Locke lays the groundwork for Hegel's philosophy of freedom becomes clear.

Tarcov's account of the spirited rhetoric surrounding the American Declaration of Independence gives a great deal of support to Lowenthal's contention that Locke is the source of the justification of national wars of liberation, at least insofar as the American regime can be understood to have a Lockean foundation or inspiration. But where Tarcov thinks that the Declaration allows prudent men to judge whether violations of rights constitute merely "light and transient causes" or evidence of a design for depotism, Lowenthal argues that Locke's argument on conquest justifies national wars of liberation at any time, in any place.

Counteracting the Effects of Bourgeoisification

If modern regimes reveal their spirited foundations in their revolutionary origins, as both Lowenthal and Tarcov suggest, the question nevertheless arises how or whether peoples maintain their spirited love of liberty after their revolutionary fervor fades. Independence attained, will a people not settle down to the business of maximizing its comfortable self-preservation? Hegel saw the problem, Michael Gillespie observes, and explicitly tried to respond.

Hegel directly contrasts the modern understanding of freedom with the ancient understanding of spiritedness as mastery. Even more than Homer, Hegel shows the connection between human freedom and man's self-conscious confrontation with death. By risking his life rather than serving another, Hegel argues, the master demonstrates his freedom from natural desire or need.

There are important differences, however, between Hegel's explication of the master-slave relation and the moral code (or understanding) of the Homeric heroes. In the first place, Homer explicitly brings the hero's choice of honor rather than mere preservation into question in the *Odyssey* when Achilles announces it is better to be a slave on earth than a king in Hades. In both the *Iliad* and the *Odyssey*, Achilles reminds his auditors that a dead man cannot enjoy either the honor or the goods he amasses through conquest. Homer suggests that it is ultimately the love and loyalty of true companionship (the *philia* of Achilles and Patrocles in the *Iliad*, of Odysseus and Penelope in the *Odyssey*) that makes human life worth living. Schooled in hardship, as well as in Hades, Odysseus rejects the nymph Calypso's offer of immortal bliss to return home to his mortal wife. Friendship is not really possible between mortal and immortal, he has discovered, because no immortal can experience and therefore understand the suffering and the uncertainty of mortal life. Through his travels Odysseus learns not only that his fate is in the hands of the gods but also that the only source of consolation is human and thus he should cling to it. Homer shows that one need not be a hero to live a good life. Like Eumaios, a slave can also be a good man, because even a slave can be god-fearing and loyal. Where Achilles wins glory he comes to disdain, Odysseus acquires wisdom and lives long and happily.[18]

Hegel explored love as a possible ground of reconciliation between self and other in his early writings, Gillespie reports, but he found it inadequate. When Hegel suggests that the life of a slave is ultimately superior to that of his master, it is not at all because he accepts his fate or the limits of human existence. On the contrary, the slave proves to be superior to his master in the long run because, prodded by fear of the master's whip, the slave works to transform the external world to suit the master's needs and desires. Where Homer celebrates the wisdom of accepting the limits of human life, Hegel glorifies the technological transformation of nature as the proof of human freedom. Hegel points toward Martin Heidegger's conclusion that technological society is a necessary product of the development of Western rationalism, because Western rationalism constitutes an attempt to reorder and so to remake the world.

If, as Homer suggests, human spiritedness manifests itself most fundamentally in rebellion against the natural limitations of human life, that is, death, then, as both Gillespie and Werner Dannhauser indicate, modern political philosophy itself is an emphatic expression of this spiritedness. Hegel steps back from the nihilistic conclusions that flow from the attempt to transform human life entirely, but, Gillespie observes, Hegel's political solution unfortunately does not work.

Where economic activity serves human desires and is inherently slavish, Hegel observes, the state represents the concrete embodiment of man's right to be recognized as an essentially free, rational being. Like Plato, Hegel insists on drawing a sharp distinction between economic exchange (or civil society, as he calls the extensive system of division of labor characteristic of modern societies) on the one hand, and political rule, or the spirited assertion of one's rightful independence, on the other. The problem is that human beings come to recognize their essential freedom from nature only in the context of a complex economy that operates generally to create and serve ever-expanding human needs; and the pressures of contending economic interests and classes operating through representative legislative institutions tend to make the state into a mere arbiter among, if not wholly subordinate to, these interests. To emphasize the independence of the state and recognition of rights, Hegel insists on the need for a hereditary monarch and professional bureaucracy, who not being elected are free from the pressures of immediate, particularistic popular desires. But he recognizes that such institutional devices will not suffice to keep the spirit of liberty alive in the people. War will also be necessary, periodically, to remind them not only that all goods are transitory but also that the state is the only real guarantor of their rights.

Although Hegel argues that the experience of war is necessary to remind people of the true ground and character of their liberty, he also thinks that war must be strictly limited. If at all possible, he advises, war should be fought by professional soldiers, not a citizen army. If the people as a whole fight, they could discover that war is a way of acquiring property and so subvert the defense of independence or sovereignty in the pursuit of gain. Hegel saw that popularizing the war effort threatened also to produce fanaticism like the Reign of Terror of the French Revolution, which destroys rather than reasserts human rights.

On the Spirited Essence of
Modern Political Philosophy

Unfortunately, wars have not remained the limited battles aimed at the reassertion of sovereign rights of independent nations that Hegel envisioned. We remain faced with the question of the place of spiritedness in modern thought and the modern state.

The first advantage of looking at contemporary politics in terms of spiritedness is that it brings to light an aspect of modern political life that tends to be neglected in contemporary liberal discourse. In the debate between John Rawls and Robert Nozick about foundations of a truly just liberal state and the extent of its power, for example, the question is discussed in terms of incentives and indifference curves, that is, the political question is reduced to a matter of economic calculation. The classic political philosophers see human beings as not content merely with material satisfaction. Human beings want more; and it is this rather undefined desire for more that provokes political as opposed to economic action.

Both this inchoate desire to get something more out of life than merely material satisfaction and man's spirited reaction to its inevitable frustration are explicitly connected, in both ancient and modern writings, to man's freedom from natural order and his consequent desire to establish political order for himself. Spiritedness is also explicitly connected, by Hobbes and Hegel as well as by Homer and Plato, to man's foreknowledge of his death. It is perhaps not surprising that man's spirited rebellion against the prospect of his own death seems to be the root of human religious hopes and fears, especially about the afterlife, as well as of political organization, even though certain of these religious beliefs threaten to undermine political order altogether. One—if not the primary political function of philosophy—according to both Aristotle and Hobbes, is to dampen some of the most dangerous forms of religious enthusiasm by showing that man's desire to perpetuate his particular, corporeal existence has no foundation in reason or experience. To this extent both ancient and modern philosophers agree that spirit needs to be disciplined by reason. Unfortunately reason alone is too weak.

The need for a spirited defense of citizens' lives and property is the ground of the modern attempt to identify spiritedness with love of liberty, as well as with the institution of a ruling class in Socrates' "city in speech." One of the many problems with the parallel between the parts of the soul and the parts of the city in the *Republic* is that as a part (indeed, the central or mediating part) of the soul, thymos presumably exists in all human beings; yet Socrates confines the expression of this characteristic to one group in the city. Insofar as the love of liberty is potentially more popular and widespread than the striving for honor, the modern association of spirit with liberty would seem to constitute a more adequate understanding than the ancient love of honor.

The tendency in modern political philosophy to identify spiritedness with love of liberty has contributed to the eclipse of our understanding of the phenomenon, if not the phenomenon itself. This is because freedom is too often taken as consisting simply of an unrestrained attempt to satisfy desires. When modern philosophers like Machiavelli and Locke explicitly try to subordinate or transform the spirited love of conquest to an equally spirited love of liberty, they change our understanding not only of the purpose or end of political association but also of the relation between philosophy and politics.

When the pursuit of political power is popularly understood primarily in terms of honor, men compete to show that they possess the qualities most praised in their particular society and thus are entitled to rule. Participation in political life (or the contest for rule) is, as a result, understood primarily in terms of the formation of character.[19] Since, as Aristotle observes (*Politics* 1257b–1258a), most human beings prize security and material comfort, the qualities praised include the martial virtues, which serve not only to defend the homeland but also to enrich it through conquest of others. Machiavelli notes that ancient statesmen are almost always generals. Nevertheless, these generals do not think they have a right to rule merely because they cater to the base desires of the populace for safety and comfort; on the contrary, they believe they ought to rule on account of their superior nobility. Because relatively few people are free from the demands of earning a living, even in ancient democracies political competition is effectively limited to the wealthy. There are rather sharp class divisions, and spiritedness is, in fact, evidenced only by a few.

When modern political philosophers attempt to check the

love of dominion with love of liberty, they not only generalize spiritedness by popularizing it (potentially expanding its scope), but they also change people's understanding of the end of politics. No longer does the polity serve primarily to inculcate virtue; on the contrary, its aim is now explicitly limited to the defense, if not extension of people's lives and property. Both Locke and Adam Smith are famous for suggesting that the people's interest will generally be better served through economic exchange than through war, and so both thinkers contribute to the tendency toward bourgeoisification that Cropsey and Gillespie observe. Nevertheless, modernity contains another, contrary direction, because of the changed relation between philosophy and spiritedness as the ground of political life.

In Plato's *Republic*, philosophy emerges as the only force or pursuit capable of checking the tyrannous tendencies of the spirited love of dominion. Rulers will not be just unless they are deprived of all privacy and particularistic attachments; and the philosopher is the only man whose activity actually frees him from such attachments. (The love of wealth tends to be fused and confused with love of liberty and love of one's own in antiquity as well as modernity.) Aristotle criticizes Plato for not paying sufficient attention to man's love of his own. He tries to moderate the love of dominion by attaching it to the love of progeny rather than to an extremely rare appreciation of the beauty of the eternal ideas. The political function of Aristotelian philosophy, however, is also to moderate or check political ambition.

The political function of philosophy changes altogether with Machiavelli, when it becomes intentionally and explicitly "inspiriting." Rather than demonstrate the limited ways in which human beings can realize their desire for immortality, modern philosophers urge their readers to undertake vast, worldly projects—not merely to assert their own liberty and to claim political dominion over further lands and oceans, but even, with the emergence of modern natural science, to reorder the natural world itself. Where ancient regimes regarded philosophy as an antagonistic, inherently suspicious, antipolitical activity (and often persecuted thinkers), modern regimes have their patron authors or defenders. That is, modern politics is obviously ideological, infused with theoretical claims and counterclaims, in a way premodern regimes never were.

Nietzsche points to the distinctive character of modern philosophy, as Dannhauser notes, when he describes it all as will to power. (Nietzsche's references to Machiavelli are all complimentary.)[20] By examining the history of political philosophy in terms of its relation to spiritedness, however, we discover that what Nietzche claims is true of philosophy in itself is true only of modern philosophy. Human beings have long been torn between an attachment to the here-and-now and the desire for something more, as Homer shows in Achilles. But the vacillation between a materialistic self-satisfaction and a rebellious reaction, which would nihilistically destroy what it cannot replace rather than see human life become more and more narrowly egoistical, has become progressively more extreme with modern philosophy's exaggerated view of the extent of human power. Like Achilles, all human beings face the prospect of their own death and thus the question of how they should live in view of that unalterable fact. Rather than seek ways to postpone or avoid contemplation of our fate through the further development of modern medicine, Nietzsche challenges his readers to show what is worthy of affirmation and preservation in human life, with all its limitations. The will to power is not Nietzsche's last word; it gives way to the doctrine of the eternal return—an affirmation the everything that has happened is so good that it should be willed to recur.

By examining the roots of dissatisfaction with contemporary liberalism in the history of modern philosophy through the lens of spiritedness, we thus come to a new understanding both of the history or development of Western philosophy and its relation to political life. The fundamental dilemma of human existence is again brought to light. If the human spirit consists, as Homer suggests, of repressed rebellion against mortality, that spirit is inherently ambiguous. A reaction against the fundamental limit on human life, it is a persistent source or expression of dissatisfaction. As the desire to continue to live, corporeally, with all our particular characteristics and despite all our individual limitations, this spirit is essentially affirmative. It seems that we have not yet learned to mediate between these spiritual extremes. Such mediation must again become recognized as the true task of both philosophy and politics.

Notes

1. Joseph Cropsey, *Political Philosophy and the Issues of Politics* (Chicago: University of Chicago Press, 1977).
2. In translating thymos as *spiritedness* I have followed the practice of Allan Bloom, *The Republic of Plato* (New York: Basic Books, 1968). As Bloom observes, "*Thymos* is the principle or seat of anger or rage. It might well be translated by that pregnant word 'heart,' which mirrors the complexity of the Greek" (p. 449). As the seat of intense feeling, thymos can thus also be translated *soul*. Since in the *Republic* Socrates treats thymos as part of the soul, in contrast to desire (*epithymia*) and the ability to calculate (*logismos*), thymos clearly cannot be translated *soul* in this context. The plurality of translations indicates the difficulty of specifying the meaning of the word.
3. In the *Cratylus* 419d–e, Socrates suggests that desire *(epithymia)* is the name given to the power that goes into the soul (thymos). And thymos has its name from the raging *(thysis)* and boiling of the soul (H. N. Fowler, trans., Loeb Classical Library, vol. 167, p. 123). The greater the desire that is frustrated, the more one's anger is fueled.
4. Aristotle *(Politics* 1297b) also observes that determination of the composition of the citizen body has in fact, although not necessarily as a matter of right, historically been determined by which part(s) of the city bear arms.
5. Having struggled to keep himself from looking at a row of corpses left by the public executioner, Leontius finally gives in to his desire and reproaches his eyes by saying, "Look, you damned wretches, take your fill of the fair sight" (440a).
6. *Politics* 1260b27–1264b25.
7. *Phaedrus* 229e–230a.

8. Homer himself teaches that such hopes are misplaced. When Zeus considers saving his son Sarpedon from death in battle in the *Iliad* XVI.433–38, Hera responds: "Most dread son of Kronos, what is this you have said? A man is a mortal long predestined to his lot, do you wish to snatch back from mournful death" (440–43). So gods and mortals not be confused, Zeus lets Sarpedon die. Nevertheless, through his graphic depiction of the Olympian gods, the poet encourages the belief that corporeal immortality is possible and so sustains man's irrational desire to perpetuate his particular bodily existence after death. Although the heroes of the Trojan War are doomed to go to Hades, Heracles is said in *Odyssey* XI to live on Olympus with the gods; these gods obviously enjoy physical pleasures, even if they are immortal. Cf. the story of Ares and Aphrodite retold in both the *Iliad* and the *Odyssey*.

9. *Discourses* II:ii. I am indebted for this particular translation to Nathan Tarcov.

10. *Prince* XV.

11. *Prince* IX; *Discourses* I:i–ii, xlvi–lix.

12. *Prince* XIX.

13. Cf. Machiavelli's praise of Hiero of Syracuse in *Prince* VI and XIII.

14. With election, the source of public honor becomes perfectly clear. The people shall judge. Machiavelli is neither the first nor the last to see how easily common people can be misled by false promises. Having little nobility and less direct experience with the responsibilities of high office, they are often not the best judges of the character of various candidates (cf. Alexis de Tocqueville, *Democracy in America* I:5, for the reasons men of fine character may also refuse to campaign for office). The people can, therefore, be manipulated through elections—in the short run, at least. Nevertheless, Machiavelli observes, where there are elections, it is almost always in the interest of ambitious men to point out the defects of those currently in office (*Discourses* I:xlvii–lv). It will, therefore, be difficult to keep malfeasance secret for long. The people may not know whether their leader is truly wise or good, moreover, but they definitely know whether they themselves are oppressed or prospering. If they do not always recognize the best and choose him, they do certainly know enough to throw "the bums" out. By instituting an electoral system, Machiavelli suggests, one thereby creates a certain kind of public morality, based not on teaching or preaching but rather on mutual self-interest. All candidates for office

vie to show how they can better serve the public, and the people reward those leaders they think have or will best foster popular interests (cf. *Democracy in America* II:ii:4, although Tocqueville clearly thinks that religion remains necessary as well). The people thus judge virtue in the same instrumental way as Machiavelli.

15. In *Prince* X, Machiavelli observes: "The cities of Germany are very free, have little countryside, and obey the emperor when they want to; they do not fear either him or any other power around, because they are so well fortified that everyone thinks their capture would be toilsome and difficult. For all of them have suitable ditches and walls, and sufficient artillery; they always keep in their public stores enough to drink and eat and to burn for a year. Besides this, so as to keep the plebs fed without loss to the public, they always keep in common supply enough to be able to give them work for a year in employments that are the nerve and the life of that city and of the industries from which the plebs is fed. They still hold military exercises in repute, and they have many institutions to maintain them." (Harvey C. Mansfield, trans. [Chicago: University of Chicago Press, 1985], pp. 43–44) Germany is the only modern nation with free communities, Machiavelli observes in *Discourses* I:lv, II:ii. The absence of freedom in modern times would seem to be a result of the Roman conquest that established the conditions for the spread of Christianity. Although in *Discourses* II:iv Machiavelli describes the Tuscan federation (whose history he fabricates for the purpose) as the second-best way of aggrandizing a republic, in contrast to Roman conquests, we note that unlike Rome, federations do not threaten the liberty of their members or neighbors. Federation would thus seem preferable on the grounds of liberty and safety, if not empire. Anyone who compares Montesquieu's *Considerations on the Causes of the Greatness of the Romans and Their Decline* with the *Discourses* will see what great influence Machiavelli had on the major proponent of federation, a constitutional separation of powers, and commerce.

16. II *Treatise* I.17, 23.

17. I *Treatise* I.10; *Treatise* II.34, 107, 111, 199, 230.

18. See Jenny Strauss Clay, *The Wrath of Athena* (Princeton: Princeton University Press, 1983) for an extremely helpful study of the *Odyssey*. The reading presented here is, however, the author's own.

19. Aristophanes' play, *The Frogs*, shows the extent to which all aspects of public life were understood in terms of the formation of character

in fifth-century Athens, when Aeschylus, the champion of traditional heroic virtue, and Euripides, the champion of democratic
loquacity and skepticism, each claim that he is the best tragedian
because his plays teach, that is, improve the character of the citizen
body. Nothing could be further from the modern understanding
of art for art's sake.

20. For example, *Beyond Good and Evil*, sec. 28; *Will to Power*, nn. 211.
304, 776, 925; *Twilight of the Idols*, "What I Owe the Ancients,"
sec. 2.

ARLENE W.
SAXONHOUSE

II

Thymos, Justice, and Moderation of Anger in the Story of Achilles

Homeric man lives in a world devoid of cosmic order. The immortal gods are divided by conflicts that often translate into war among men. Like men, they are subject to forces—passions and the Fates—that they themselves do not understand and over which they have no control. Men cannot turn to the gods for a universal structure to give order and meaning to their lives. Righteousness cannot come from gods so fickle and powerless. Instead, men must establish their own rules of righteousness concerning what is due to others and to themselves and defining the nature and the order of their communities. And as the gods are not always present, men themselves must enforce these rules. It is man's *thymos*, his spirited sense of what is right, of what brings honor and glory, that defends and preserves these rules of order. When that order is threatened, when the laws of distribution are not followed, man in his anger will attempt to reimpose structure on the world. The community of men relies in part on the spirited defense of the distribution of goods and fame. Without this order, life is a chaotic morass, empty of meaning, with man little more than a plaything of the gods, passing quickly through life as do the leaves of the forest.

The thymos in defense of justice—what is due—preserves a tenuous stability in human affairs. The spirited insistence on what is owed is the guardian of justice for men who cannot rely on the gods.[1] Yet, at the same time that the thymos preserves the order of man's existence within his own community, the thymos of a man like Achilles reveals ambiguities in the justice he spiritedly pursues. What is due—honor or booty or power—is never clearly prescribed; bestowing harms or benefits can never exactly match the injuries or services rendered. The ascription of authority cannot rest on precise definitions of worth. While honor and legitimacy lie at the foundation of the political community, the hero is never adequately honored, nor is the legitimacy of the ruler unassailable. Values other than justice and its defense are part of the human social experience. In thymetic pursuit of justice, paying back what is owed, granting honor to those who have pursued it, or obedience to the "true" ruler carried to its extreme may threaten the community. The demands of the thymos for justice or legitimacy can never be met. Consequently, a moderation of the defense of what is due in human affairs is necessary. The story of Achilles is of a man who learns to moderate, but not to abandon, his expectations of what is due. While he will never see the legitimacy in the claims to authority of an inferior Agamemnon, by the end of the epic he will set human experience in the context of a disordered world. In his grief he learns to accept human experience, not as it is, but in its limited capacity to be ordered by man.

At the beginning of the *Iliad*, Achilles insists upon the general principle that the best warrior should receive recognition in the form of booty for his deeds of courage on the battlefield. Agamemnon demands a prize to replace Chryseis, the girl taken from him. He does not say that it will be Achilles' prize. Achilles rises to the defense of what has been allotted. He is angered by Agamemnon's love of possessions (he calls him *philokteanotate*, I.122) and by the disruption of the established distribution of prizes and goods. The great-spirited (*megathymoi*, I. 135) Achaeans have no more to give. At this point Agamemnon proposes that he receive the prize of some other prince, Achilles or Ajax or Odysseus. It is only after Achilles again lashes out at Agamemnon's inequitable distribution of goods (characteristic of earlier times) and threatens to leave Troy that Agamemnon claims Achilles' prize, Bryseis, to compensate for Chryseis.

The conflict between the two men is not over the prize or

the loss of Achilles' esteem because Bryseis has been taken from
him, but over the failure of Agamemnon to protect the principles
of distribution governing the actions of the men of Troy. Achilles
lived by the principles articulated in the famous passage in which
Sarpedon asks: "Why are we honored especially with special
seats and cuts of meat and full cups . . . so that all look upon us
as gods?" The answer is: "So that we going forward with the
foremost ranks may stand having our share of the blazing battle"
(XII.310–11, 315–16). Prowess in battle is requited with visible
rewards that all acknowledge and admire.[2] The warrior fights
for these as he fights for his community, be it the conglomerate
of nations that comprise the Achaean army or the city of Troy.
The rewards are expected for services performed on the field of
battle. According to Agamemnon, however, distribution is not
to be made according to individual worth in battle.[3] Achilles'
thymos is aroused at this perversion of the principles that underlie
his perception of the necessary structure and expectations of the
community at war.[4] At first, the spirited defense of these principles calls forth the sword, but Athene restrains him. Instead,
Achilles turns to words: "Never do I have a prize equal to yours
. . . but the greater part of furious war my hands manage. Whenever the distribution of spoils comes, to you belongs the far
greater prize, while I weary from fighting carry to the ships
some small dear thing" (I.163–186). Denied what he deserves
and with the principles that he sees as necessary for the community to keep its warriors fighting undermined, Achilles announces to the assembled Achaeans: "Now I go home to Phthia"
(I.169).

At the assembly, Achilles' response to Agamemnon had
been so passionate as to need divine restraint. When he retires
from both the assembly of men and the battlefield, his leisure
gives him time to reflect on the meaning and adequacy of the
system of distributive justice according to which he sought what
is owed. Achilles broods while battles rage, Diomedes slaugh-
ters, and Trojans advance. He comes to a generalized dissatisfaction with a world in which the human definition of justice,
of expectations and payments, is inadequate. Recognizing the

inadequacy of justice, of the principles defining what is owed or due, his thymos is stifled. Achilles feels grief rather than anger at the loss of what he had pursued.

Agamemnon in his turn learns the consequences of ruling with scant notice to what his warriors expect. The warriors will not fight when the principles under which they had previously fought and which had provided an order to their world are not in force. With the withdrawal of the greatest warrior, Achilles, the army as a whole suffers. The response of Agamemnon, no longer able to mobilize his army, is retreat; he forsakes the glory and victory promised him (owed him?) by the gods. The spirited Diomedes insists on staying and fighting, on not yielding the honor and glory of conquest. But it is the wise old Nestor who seeks to draw Achilles back into battle by reestablishing the principles violated earlier. Nestor, arguing that wisdom should be the basis of persuasion, proposes that many gifts and sweet words (IX.74–75) be sent to Achilles to appease his anger.

At last Agamemnon acknowledges the failure of the principles by which he had sought to rule. These principles had led him to act "blindly" (IX.115–116, 119). He now proposes to accept the standard of worth above status that rewards the warrior and acknowledges the army's dependence on the hero's efforts. He states, "I wish to make amends and give countless reparations" (IX.120). He proceeds to enumerate these countless gifts—thirty-five lines worth of tripods, women, and land—to pay back Achilles and to lure him back into the community of men governed by principles of distribution that attend the military worth.[5]

The embassy of Odysseus, Phoenix, and Ajax proceeds to the tent of Achilles, where Odysseus repeats the thirty-five lines of countless gifts, but Achilles is not longer to be drawn into the world of compensation. As he understands it now, the world of which he had been a part never functioned according to its articulated principles—and indeed never could.[6] Achilles says, "There was not any thanks for men always fighting without pause" (IX.316–17). Man's efforts to preserve order cannot be founded on a claim to justice, which cannot be perfected. The precision that the thymos of Achilles demands in giving and receiving what is due accords little with the experience of men at war and peace. Achilles raises questions about the meaning of a war in which the definition of what is one's own is unclear; about the possibility of Agamemnon compensating a warrior as great as Achilles; and about the adequacy of agreed-upon rewards as payment for success in battle, where men face death. For, beyond what any community can give to the men who fight well, "The same lot awaits the one remaining at home and the one who fights exceptionally hard. In the same honor we are, the cowardly and the brave" (IX.318–19). Achilles has a new perspective on the social life of man, differing from the justice he had pursued before related to compensation for the defense of his friends. Now the process of distribution lies outside human influence. The distribution on which he now focuses is not limited to the Achaeans but applies to Achaean and Trojan alike: "The man who performs nothing and the man who has performed many deeds both die" (IX. 320). Agamemnon as a king among men no longer holds the reins of distribution; thus his attempt at compensation fails. There can be no compensation for death. The motivating principles that Achilles' thymos previously defended have disappeared.

Achilles' thymos previously demanded that the community acknowledge his distinctive value and demonstrate through its gifts his superiority to other men on the field of battle. Now Achilles is overwhelmed by the fundamental equality of all men in death and sees no point in the distinctions a community can make. His vision, in expanding beyond the community, questions the fundamental principles on which the community is based. Under the principles of universal equality in which no distinctions are made according to worth, the spirit of Achilles is not only moderated, it is killed. He is no longer the warrior as he prepares to head home to Phthia, yielding the fame and prizes he had fought for.

Odysseus appeals to Achilles according to the explicit terms of Achilles' withdrawal from battle. He recites the long list of treasures meant to compensate Achilles and quotes Peleus,

Achilles' father, to the effect that Achilles should moderate his
"greathearted *thymos*" and show a love of gentleness (*philophro-
sune*, IX.255–56). The thymos leads to conflict, Peleus had
warned; instead of being a principle of order, it created conditions
under which order was impossible—as was the case in the camp
of the Achaeans. Phoenix in his long-winded speech articulates
factors other than distributions that might motivate warriors;
particularly, loyalty to family. Ajax follows suit and brings in
friendship toward the suffering Achaeans and specifically for the
three who have traveled to his tent—those who are *philtatoi* to
him (IX.641). Achilles replies briefly, in contrast to his response
to Odysseus—too briefly in his simple dismissal of family and
friendship as motivation for action. He focuses on hatred of the
king rather than love of his friends. For the love, care, and
friendship that can be shown through action on the field of battle,
Phoenix promises Achilles that the Achaeans will honor him as
a god (IX.603, also Odysseus at line 297). Achilles, though,
knows he can never be equal to a god; he is mortal. With no
reason to die sooner in battle, he chooses to die later—at home.[7]

After the failure of the embassy to bring Achilles back into
battle, Ajax describes Achilles: "That cruel man, he has made
harsh the greathearted *thymos* within his breast, unmoved by the
love of his companions . . . a pitiless man" (IX.628–32). Achilles'
state is the result of his disillusionment with principles that he
now finds meaningless. He says, "For me whatever they say to
be the wealth of Troy cannot be of equal worth to human life"
(IX.401). He is pitiless because he can see no compatibility between facing death in battle and the rewards one may expect for
courage. Death will always come. Ajax's accusation is justified
insofar as it applies to Achilles as an Achaean, but Ajax does not
understand that Achilles has moved beyond the community of
the Achaeans to pity all men. Achilles does care for his friends,
but he recognizes that care ultimately cannot keep those he loves
alive. Even his mother, an immortal, cannot stave off death for
her son.

The change in Achilles is vividly illustrated by his changed
attitude toward Bryseis, the prize taken by Agamemnon. At

first, she is a prize, a gift from the Achaeans in compensation for Achilles' success in war. When she is taken from Achilles, his honor and respect are diminished before the Achaeans. Now he presents the relationship with Bryseis as one of love: she is not merely what is owed to him, but one with whom he is capable of having a loving and fond relationship. To the distress of many an editor, he uses the term *alochon* (wife) to describe her—his dear wife (IX.336). He asks of the sons of Atreus: "Do they alone of mortal men love their wives?" (IX.340). Achilles follows this rhetorical question with the comment, "Whoever is a good man and has his wits about him loves her who is his own, as I myself love her [Bryseis] with my heart (thymos) even though she was taken by the sword" (IX.341–43). For the warrior, Bryseis exists as a sign of martial greatness. For the man that Achilles has become—by confronting death off the battlefield and recognizing his community with all mortal men—Bryseis is no longer defined by her relation to warlike actions. The thymos, no longer defending what is one's own according to suspect principles, abstracts from the question of distribution. The care is for what is one's own, what one has grown to love as one's own, and not what is owed to one. Achilles, however, will discover that the principles underlying the community he now rejects are necessary to preserve what one loves as one's own; he is about to suffer the death of Patroclus. His rejection of the values of justice expressed by the community as inadequate turns him toward the love of one's own, the desire to return home, and the love of a captive maiden, illustrating his rejection of the warrior ethic. Yet the death of Patroclus shows that Achilles cannot easily discard the warrior ethic; while death is the fate of all, he learns that his own actions can precipitate the death of those he loves.

Achilles' vision of a retreat from the world of inadequate justice is aborted when his beloved is killed. The thymos, which has been focused on the failure to receive the goods due to Achilles, is redirected against those who have caused him harm. He is drawn back into the battle, not because of pity for his suffering companions, but because he now must give what is due. He must act and seek revenge on Hector. Achilles' anger is not restrained by the gods, nor is it limited to words, as in his response to Agamemnon; the gods now support his fury, and glorious arms are forged for him in the fires of Hephaestos.

Achilles, however, remains distant from the community of the Achaeans. He has seen the inadequacy of the principles of distribution according to military worth when death awaits all. Agamemnon, in a long mea culpa speech, repeats his offer of countless gifts. Achilles responds with indifference: "Whether you are willing to give the gifts, as is seemly or to hold on to them, that is up to you" (XIX.147–48). The gifts are no longer of issue for Achilles; he had dismissed them earlier in his response to the embassy (IX.378). His thymos no longer seeks to preserve what is his own according to the now meaningless standards of the community. His aim is to engage in battle, and avenge the death of his friend. Agamemnon, delighted at the reconciliation, is ready to yield the gifts immediately, misconstruing the meaning of Achilles' return to battle. Achilles demurs: "Another time rather you ought to labor about this," he tells Agamemnon, ". . . when the anger in my breast is not so great" (XIX.200–02).

Achilles is not willing even to pause, as Odysseus says men must, for food and drink. He says, "Do not bid me sate my heart with grain nor wine, since dread grief comes" (XIX.306–07). The psychological motives and the physical necessities that govern the Achaeans are irrelevant for Achilles. His thymos no longer sets him within the structure of human society. The vengeance he seeks goes beyond the boundaries of the laws of camp and body. Nothing could please his thymos but engagement in the "mouth of bloody war" (XIX.313). He fights now with a pained thymos driven to bring harm to him who has caused him harm. His earlier insistence on what is due to the

good warrior had defined him as part of the community of men
bound by agreements and expectations. In his rage against those
who have harmed him, he transcends humanity.[8]

Achilles sets off to battle fortified by divine food, closer to
the gods than to men. He carries on a conversation with his horse
in which he acknowledges his imminent death (XIX.421). In
Book IX, we saw Achilles immobilized by the vision of death and
the inadequacy of a system unable to compensate the warrior.
Death had been faced in earlier battles with the uncertainty of
whether courage would be repaid; the suppressed anger about
that uncertainty surfaced in Achilles' first confrontation with
Agamemnon. Now, he fights to give what is due to his enemy.
Death is openly embraced (this is necessary to ensure the justice
of revenge), and his return to battle is marked by an acceptance
of death (XXI.110), a transcendence of the body (also characterized by his refusal to eat). He rages across the Trojan plain rising
first as a shining star and then descending as a lion slaying warrior
after warrior, as he searches for the one he must kill. The anger
against Hector is an anger against all the Trojans: "And you [Tro-
jans] will suffer an evil fate until all of you pay for the death of
Patroclus and the grief of the Achaeans" (XXI.133).

Before the lofty walls of Troy the two heroes meet. Hector
proposes an agreement: The victor will return the body of the
defeated warrior for a ransom. The gods are to stand as witnesses
(XXII.254–59). Hector imagines a world of rational converse,
controlled by words, where reason limits deeds and gods enforce
oaths. Achilles acts not out of reason or calculation. Had he done
so he would have been on the curved ships sailing toward Phthia.
Achilles talks of animals, of lions and wolves exhibiting no *hom-
ophrona thymon* (spirit that comes to agreement). The spirit of
Achilles ties him to the beasts, but while the beasts kill for food,
Achilles kills "so that now you will pay back the full price of
the griefs of my comrades" (XXII.271–72). The human spirit in
the pursuit of vengeance is not the same as animal passions. The
thymos envisions a world in which an order can be established,
in which an evil deed can be repaid. To Hector's proposal for a
covenant (*harmononian*, XXII.255), Achilles responds: "Dog, do

not implore me by my knees or your parents! Would that anger and *thymos* might somehow move me to cut apart your limbs and eat your flesh raw, such things have I suffered from you" (XXII.346–47). The violence of the image does not undermine the underlying order, which presupposes that one action can account or pay for another.

Achilles wishes he could tear Hector apart and eat his flesh raw, but he does not, for he is neither lion nor wolf. He does not kill for food. He kills in affirmation against the chaos of the world. He had not found order in the camp of the Achaeans, in the gifts proferred to the best warrior. Among the Achaeans, others supplied the order; here, on the battlefield, he applies the order with his own sense of what is due. Killing Hector is the act of a man, not a beast; it asserts the human capacity to structure a world that the gods do not. The covenant proposed by Hector relied upon the gods for its enforcement. Achilles relies only on himself. The spirited hero of the *Iliad* understands, as Hector does not, the inadequacy of oaths sworn before the gods. The vengeance Achilles seeks must be his own.

Achilles, though not the flesh-eating beast he imagines in his speech, does leave Hector's body for dogs and birds to devour; the body of his enemy remains unwashed and unwept. Achilles' anger asserts itself in the "unseemly" (*aeikea*, XXIII.24) treatment of the body.[9] Achilles drags the body, with its face in the dust, behind his chariot. Achilles' anger does not cease with the death of Hector. His unmoderated thymos, driven to assert human standards of vengeance, prevents him from rejoining the community of men. No punishment to Hector or his corpse can compensate for the loss of Patroclus, just as no gift from Agamemnon could pay for all that Achilles accomplishes in war. Justice among men can never be perfect. Achilles, passionate in his pursuit of justice, must be made to moderate his spirit by outside forces (the gods), just as Athene had transformed his anger at Agamemnon into words.

The lack of moderation in Achilles' treatment of Hector's body also marks his grief over the death of Patroclus. Straight

from battle, he leads the Myrmidons in lamentation: "When we
have taken our fill of grievous lamentation, we will unharness
our horses and dine here all together" (XXIII.9–10). But Achilles
never joins the feast—nor does he wash the bloody gore from
his body as the other men do. He goes off to the beaches, where
his groans fill the air. The demands of the body finally catch up
with the spirit of Achilles and sleep overcomes him. It is during
this sleep that the vision of Patroclus reminds him that burial
must take place, indicating that grief has its limits. This vision
recalls Achilles to life despite its imperfections.

The burial, and the funeral games with Achilles presiding,
mark the gradual return of Achilles to the community of men
and the moderation of his thymos. The funeral games are the
highly stylized competitions for honors, prizes, and glory, in
which the deserts are preestablished. Achilles as organizer of the
games, is in charge of the distribution of prizes. In this role he
reveals the inadequacy of precise models of prize winning. Principles other than those originally established may be appropriate.
He must moderate the conflicts that arise when the original principles are replaced. In the chariot race, the first prize goes to the
winner, but Achilles decided that the second prize should go to
the one who ought to have won the race but came in last. Though
the Achaeans approve, the other participants do not. They demand recognition too. Adjustments must be made, prizes re-
distributed, all for the sake of a certain harmony among men.
Achilles accomplishes all, maintaining a spirited good humor
among the participants. A spear-throwing contest at the end of
the games never takes place because it is known that Agamemnon
is the best. The prize will be given without testing him. The
worth of Meriones, not nearly so great as the king of the
Achaeans, will be recognized, and he is included among the prize
recipients. The harmony of the community honoring Patroclus
depends upon both the structure of the games, and the flexibility
of its standards. The thymos demanding perfection in distribution would threaten the order of those assembled.

Once the funeral games are over, the qualities that Achilles
demonstrates as leader fade. Grief and anger dominate Achilles:

food is rejected and Hector is again dragged around the tomb of Patroclus. The gods find Achilles' lack of moderation "unseemly." Apollo describes Achilles' madness: "Neither heart nor mind is properly ordered . . . , but as a wild lion who with great force and a headstrong *thymos* goes among the sheep of mortals to take his feast" (XXIV.40–43).[10] Achilles' continued harshness transforms him into an outsider and predator among men, not bound by reason or compassion. So intent is Achilles on revenge that he has, in Apollo's words, "cast off pity, nor is there any shame to him" (XXIV.44–45). Hera tries to prevent any honor for Hector's corpse, but Zeus seeks to have it returned to Priam, for "of the mortals who lie in Ilios Hector was the most beloved by the gods" (XXIV.66–67, see 33–34). Hector had offered Zeus many feasts at the altar. Though Zeus will not condone the theft of the corpse planned by some of the gods, he will send Thetis to her son, and Iris to Priam, to set the stage for the return of Hector's body and the cessation of the grief and madness of Achilles.

The passion of Achilles does not allow him to set limits on himself. Only the force of Zeus' will brings an end to his weeping and to his treatment of Hector. For Achilles, the end can never come by itself. When Thetis comes as a messenger from Zeus, Achilles agrees to the limit established by the gods and to ransom the body of Hector. He yields, since the king of the gods "with ready *thymos* . . . reveals it" (XXIV.140). Achilles responds to Thetis, "So be it." Obedient to the gods, or recognizing that he cannot fight them, he accepts that he is part of the community of mortals that ransoms as a form of exchange.

Priam, also urged on by the gods, engages in this exchange, not because the body of Hector is owed to him or because he deserves to get back what is his, but because he loves his son: "Let me die if need be, in the arms of my son," he says to those who try to hold him back from visiting Achilles (XXIV.222). Priam makes no claims concerning debts or covenants before the gods; he acts not according to a thymos demanding what is owed, but from the love of a father for his noble child. When

Priam arrives at the tent of Achilles, he confronts the young warrior at once; "Remember your father" (XXIV.486). There is no attempt to argue about the excessiveness of Achilles' revenge, no attempt to demand back the body, only the recollection of the parental ties which war has disrupted. The parallel of Peleus and Achilles and of Priam and Hector suggest the universality of relationships. Peleus will soon mourn for Achilles as Priam mourns for Hector. Priam brings countless gifts, but the emphasis is elsewhere: "Respect the gods, Achilles, and pity me; remember your father," he repeats (XXIV.503–04). Pity had often been urged on Achilles without effect. Now the thymos and the memory of his father stir him (XXIV.507). With the same hands that have slaughtered Priam's son, Achilles, gently raises the old man who had grasped his knees in supplication, and they grieve for those they loved, Priam for Hector, Achilles for his father and for Patroclus.

Achilles ends the mourning as he takes the old man's hand and gazes upon him with pity. He says, "Although we grieve let us let go of the suffering in our *thymos*" (XXIV.522–23). Achilles blames their anguish not on mortals (Agamemnon or Hector or himself), but on the gods "who devise for us miserable mortals to live in pain while they are without cares" (XXIV.525). The greatest suffering lies in the arbitrary and capricious distribution of benefits and harms from the gods: Of the three urns on Zeus's doorstep, only one is filled with blessings; sometimes man receives from the one with blessings, sometimes from those with evils. There is no order, no reason or purpose to this distribution. Achilles from being blessed becomes one who is not. Priam once was blessed with sons and land and wealth, but then war came; the sons were killed, the land ravaged, and the wealth lost. Peleus was once happy, but he is old now and soon to lose a son (whose absence subjects him to invasion). The good are not necessarily blessed and the bad do not necessarily suffer. As Achilles sees it now, having contemplated the inadequacy of human and divine justice, as he remembers his own father and pities Priam, grieving accomplishes nothing. It is left to man to provide the order and value the gods deny.

Priam's grief will not cease until the body of Hector is returned and cared for. He demands an order and a structure, albeit a man-made one. Achilles must receive the ransom and return the body before the grief of Priam will cease. This request, though, stirs up Achilles' anger. Priam is no longer the sorrowful old man, but one who insists on a world of compensation, even though his world is tumbling down. Achilles had been motivated by the principles of compensation. The story of Achilles is partly about the failure of those principles. He had tried to pass on that understanding to Priam, but the king refuses to accept a world in which compensation and worth are ignored. He tries to impose an order Achilles knows is not there. When Achilles returns the body, it is clear that he does so not because the body is owed to Priam, but because the gods told him to do so. Achilles realizes that some god must have led Priam from the gates of Troy to the Achaeans' camp. (XXIV. 561–67). Achilles' diffidence in this act of return and the thymos straining to reassert itself (XXIV. 568–70, 585–86) suggests that the debt will never be fully settled; the harm will never be commensurate with all he has suffered and the grief will never end. The return of the body is a delicate matter, with suppressed revenge on the part of the father and of the slayer about to burst forth. But all that transpires is Achilles' speech to the ghost of Patroclus asking that he not be angry about the return of the corpse, since "the ransom did not seem unseemly" (XXIV. 594). Achilles accepts human conventions that suggest compatibility between incompatibles, between the body of an enemy and a cartload of treasures. Achilles' own story shows him the importance of compensation—and its limits.

Once Achilles accepts the conventions of exchange, he proposes food. He tells of Niobe and how, despite her grief at the loss of her six sons and six daughters, she partook of food. A meal is served, and Achilles presides over the distribution of food as he had presided over the distribution of prizes. Both mark the necessity of his return to the community of mortals.

Achilles agrees not to attack Troy during Hector's funeral. This truce is not owed, and the gods have not demanded it.

With the description of Hector's funeral, which concludes the
Iliad, we know that Achilles has kept his word. He made an
agreement much like the covenant Hector had proposed.
Achilles, though, does not call on the gods to witness this agreement as Hector had. The truce is Achilles' assertion of man's
ordering of his own world. The thymos he had shown so vividly
ensures now that at least for a short time order will remain.

Achilles is a man of overwhelming passion; his anger is
greater than other men's, and his grief exceeds human bounds.
Passion is necessary in the human conflict with the gods; but it
also threatens community. Achilles moves out of and back into
the community of mortals. He has once again eaten, and he has
once again accepted limits: limits to his anger, to his grief, and
to his expectations concerning the possibilities of justice. In the
agreement to hold off battle, he also acknowledges his commitment to battle, to reenter the world of imperfect justice and
bodily mortality. It is here that pity must take precedence over
the principles of distribution. It is pity for the lot of all men in
this world without purpose that lifts man above fame in song
and that shows us the necessary limits to our spirit. The story
of Achilles is a tale of transformation through reflection and
moderation, leading not to the abandonment of the notion of
what is due, but to the understanding of the limits of this
concept.[11]

Notes

1. The relation between the Homeric gods and justice is an ambiguous
   one that has provided fodder for many a scholarly treatment of the
   Iliad. The debate perhaps reached its peak with Hugh Lloyd-Jones's
   claims that the Justice of Zeus was there from the beginning of
   Greek literature, rejecting the views of such scholars as E. R. Dodds
   and A. W. H. Adkins. (*The Justice of Zeus* [Berkeley and Los An-
   geles: University of California Press, 1971], Sather Classical Lectures). But however much the gods, or Zeus in particular, may
   work to secure equitable distributions of goods and evils—for the
   Trojans, for Agamemnon, for Achilles, or for Priam—divine efforts

in this direction are not readily perceived by mortals nor relied upon by the participants in the Homeric epics.

2. As Adam Parry notes: "Its [Sarpedon's speech] assumption is, first, that honor can be fully embodied in the tangible expressions of it, . . . for *everyone agrees* on the meaning of these tangible expressions." "The Language of Achilles," *Transactions of the American Philological Society* 87 (1956), p. 3, italics mine.

3. In fairness to Agamemnon, we must of course acknowledge that he is acting according to his own principles of order and expectations. As ruler, according to a principle that is not entirely clear in the *Iliad* (cf. IX.39, Diomedes' speech in which he mentions the scepter granted to Agamemnon by Zeus, IX.98–99, Nestor's speech in which reference is again made to the Zeus-given scepter "so that we may take counsel," and Thucydides, I.9, where the historian mentions the superiority in ships), Agamemnon in his turn seeks to defend his authority as irrefutable and not subject to question. He took Bryseis from Achilles, though the elders opposed such an action (IX.108). Clearly, in Agamemnon's case there is a disjunction between the ascription of authority and the ability to exercise that authority; neither strength in battle nor the wisdom of age justify the scepter granted him by Zeus. Yet he defends his own principles at first. As king of the Achaeans, he sees the community of warriors as bound together by principles different from those which motivate Achilles (and Sarpedon); allegiance to the king and acceptance of his wishes provide order. Indeed, he sees in Achilles' principles a serious threat to the order he tries to preserve, for in the encouragement of the pursuit of honor for courage, Achilles' principles also encourage conflict among the leading warriors of the same army (cf. Sophocles' *Ajax* for a powerful expression of how far this difficulty pervades the Achillean ethos). We see in this conflict the underlying insecurity of a community that can be based on a different set of expectations concerning what is due and to whom; they may not only be different but as in the case of Achilles and Agamemnon they may be contradictory. The discussion that follows in this essay focuses on Achilles' understanding of the basis of human community. He is the thymetic character of the *Iliad* and while both he and Agamemnon learn to moderate their expectations, it is the passion of Achilles that dominates our reading of the poem.

4. At the same time, though, we must remember that the principles

that Achilles sees as underlying the organization of a community at war may also threaten the viability of that community. The passion with which Achilles pursues his principles in no way assures that those principles provide for a viable political structure over time. I owe the thoughts in this and the preceding footnote to comments from Catherine Zuckert.

5. Agamemnon still insists that Achilles recognize how much more kingly (*basileuteros*) he is than Achilles and that the greater age of the king deserves respect (IX.160–61). It is a passage tactfully omitted by Odysseus, but it does not undermine the critical willingness of Agamemnon to return to principles of distribution of goods based on military worth.

6. Parry, in "The Language of Achilles" (p. 6), refers to this as the distinction between seeming and being that the epic formulations could not adequately express. This alerts us as well to the relationships between Achilles and the problem of justice in the *Republic*.

7. A brief remark (IX.651 ff.) by Achilles in his reply to Ajax suggests that he might fight should the Trojans, with Hector at the forefront, approach the tents and ships of the Myrmidons, but Odysseus' report of the failure of the embassy reiterates Achilles' intention to leave and encourage others to do so as well (IX.682–83). See further Cedric Whitman, *Homer and the Heroic Tradition* (New York: W. W. Norton, 1965), pp. 190–91.

8. Mera J. Flaumenhaft, "The Undercover Hero: Odysseus from Dark to Daylight," *Interpretation* 10:1 (Jan. 1982), p. 31, elaborates on the significance of eating in this section of the *Iliad*.

9. *Aeikea* recurs frequently in describing Achilles' treatment of Hector's body. There is debate, though, as to whether *unseemly* refers to Achilles' actions as being in themselves inappropriate (or excessive) or whether the term refers to the fact that Hector's body suffers such indignities as Achilles gives it. Cf. Samuel Elliot Basset, "Achilles' Treatment of Hector's Body," *Transactions of the American Philological Society* 64 (1933), pp. 41–65.

10. Achilles is compared not only here to a lion. This image and the power of his thymos suggest further connections with the role of Thrasymachus in the *Republic*.

11. Seth Benardete, "Achilles and the *Iliad*," *Hermes* 91:1 (1963), describes the movement of the *Iliad* from "the apparently higher to the apparently lower" (p. 16). The transformation of Achilles de-

scribed above with its focus on thymos rather than opposites traces the same trajectory. We should also note that the lessons of Achilles carry us on many dimensions to fifty-century Athens, as for example in the Mytilenean debate where the high-spirited Cleon's demands for justice are countered by the moderate Diodotus (or the gift of Zeus).

MARY P.
NICHOLS

III

Spiritedness and Philosophy
in Plato's *Republic*

Although the *Republic* is an explicit attack on the Greek poets, especially Homer (378b–391e; 595a–607c), its teaching about man's political life has much in common with Homer's *Iliad*. Both works explore man's spirited attempt to maintain an orderly and just world where men receive the rewards and punishments they deserve. Achilles' defense of his community's distribution of prizes as well as his attempt to punish Hector for Patroclus' death parallels Glaucon's search for a justice choiceworthy for its own sake and for a political community characterized by justice. Spiritedness moves both Achilles and Glaucon. Both the *Iliad* and the *Republic* show the difficulty, if not impossibility, of attaining the perfect justice these men desire, for such justice requires that incommensurable aspects of human life be treated as if they were commensurable. Plato joins Homer in teaching the need for man to moderate his spiritedness.

Plato, however, shows us a dimension of spiritedness not present in the Homeric world. In the *Republic*, Glaucon turns to philosophy in order to guarantee justice, just as Socrates turns to philosophy to create the just city. Plato presents spiritedness in its union with philosophy. Spiritedness, by allying itself with philosophy, ultimately perverts philosophy and tyrannizes over human life. This tyranny is manifest in a communism that deprives its participants of individuality and in a philosophy that blinds itself to the complexity and incompleteness of the human soul. It is as cruel and self-defeating as Achilles' spiritedness that tyrannizes over Hector's corpse. Plato also suggests a new way

spiritedness can be moderated—through Socratic political philosophy, which describes the incommensurables that spiritedness
denies.

I explore the role of spiritedness in the *Republic* by discussing first the problem of the guardians, in whose nature spiritedness predominates over the gentle and philosophic elements.
This distortion of human nature is visible in Socrates' account
of the soul modeled upon the city. In both city and soul, the
close alliance of spiritedness with reason produces an undue depreciation of desire and a concomitant suppression of the particular or private dimension of human life. The self-contained
man, whose justice resides in internal rule, and the desireless
men in the city, resemble the self-sufficient ideas of the city's
rulers. It is not philosophy, however, but the spirited distortion
of philosophy that leads to such abstractions. I also discuss the
Republic's treatment of philosophy—how it is allied with spiritedness in order to serve the needs of the city.

The Guardians' Nature

The city that Socrates describes in the *Republic* faces a threat from
its soldiers: if the soldiers are harsh and cruel to their city's
enemies, will they not be so to its citizens as well? Will the
guardians of the city truly protect it? Socrates poses the question
that lies at the heart of the *Republic*: does man's defense of himself
lead him to embrace what will destroy him? Are the harsh and
spirited elements that are necessary for survival ultimately destructive of life? Can spiritedness be combined with gentleness,
for, as Socrates says, "a gentle nature is opposed to a spirited
one" (375c)?[1]

Socrates declares that the dog combines the very qualities
that seem to be opposed and that this proves they can coexist in
the same nature. A dog, Socrates observes, is gentle toward his
familiars but angry toward strangers. This characteristic of the
dog, and of the guardian who resembles it, Socrates says, is
philosophic (375a–376a). The dog distinguishes friendly looks

from the hostile looks of strangers having learned the one and being ignorant of the other. The dog, therefore, is a philosopher, "since it defines what's its own and what's alien by knowledge and ignorance" (376b).

Socrates' model of the philosophic dog for the city's guardians reveals the harsh requirements of the city more than it proves that a solution to the city's problems with the guardian is possible. Men are aware of themselves and of their separate identities, whereas dogs are not. Men rebel against authority when their dignity is at stake, while the noble dog never turns on his master even if mistreated (376a). Men are independent of their political community because they are not merely citizens. Socrates' comparison of the guardian to the dog indicates the kind of men the city needs. They must identify with their city as a whole. Like the dog, the guardians must react differently to familiars and strangers, not because they reflect on what actions are appropriate, but because they have extended their self-love to their familiars. In both their gentleness and their harshness, the guardians are protecting their own against the alien. Their different responses are thus owed to an inflexibility produced by habit or custom rather than to a flexibility given by the understanding. Socrates even admits that the dog is angry when it sees someone it doesn't know, "although it never had any bad experience with him," and greets warmly whomever it knows, "even when it never had a good experience with him" (376a).

Because the dog and the guardian react out of habit rather than understanding, it is surprising that Socrates describes them as philosophic. A philosopher can indeed define his own and the alien by knowledge and ignorance, but he does not rest content with what he already knows. He does not resemble the dog or the guardian in repelling the unknown, as if it were his enemy; rather, he is attracted to the unknown, which he is constantly trying to understand. If a man thrusts the unknown away, he never learns anything more than he already knows. If he is hostile to everything unfamiliar, he does not grow or change. Socrates is attributing a closed or static character to the philosopher in calling the guardian philosophic. By associating the philosopher with the guardian, he is giving a definition of philosophy that is consistent with the requirements of the city. This philosopher, for example, is not cruel to his own city by questioning its assumptions. On the contrary, he defends the city against aliens when they question it. Socrates introduces philosophy in the *Republic* as a support for the city.[2]

Because the noble dog possesses neither a man's sense of his independent existence nor his capacity and desire to learn, Socrates' image points to the problem of political life: given these capabilities, can men form a stable community that meets their common needs? After presenting the noble dog, Socrates sketches the education and institutions necessary to guarantee a secure and lasting community. The guardians' education makes them independent of all particular human beings in order to attach them solely to the city. They learn, for example, to feel little pain at the death of relatives and friends. Communism of property and especially communism of women and children deprive the guardians of anything that is peculiarly their own. The complete safety of the community demands that the guardians have little sense of themselves as distinct from their families. The safety of the community also necessitates curbing man's desire to know. The philosophic guardian does not extend his horizon beyond the familiar limits of the city and its opinions.

If the city's education of the guardians and its communism could accomplish its intention, the guardians would never turn on their fellow citizens for their own advantage. In this sense, they would be gentle to their own as well as cruel to strangers. But would their education and institutions succeed in balancing the harsh tendencies of spiritedness with the gentler passions? In outlining the guardians' education, Socrates counterpoises gymnastic to music: gymnastic hardens the spirited part of the guardians' nature, while music softens the philosophic part (410c ff.). By implying that the music in the guardians' education has a softening or gentling effect, however, Socrates misrepresents the effect of the music allowed in the city. Its aim is to make men hard. For example, when discussing the public tales, the core of the guardians' education in music, Socrates is concerned with

restricting the tales that made men "softer than they ought [to
be]" rather than those that made men too hard (387c). The Socrates
censors the portrayal of heroes overcome by grief or laughter
(387c–389a) and offers truthfulness and self-control as appropriate poetic models (389b–391e). Moreover, he includes the
warlike harmonies in the guardians' education in music (399a).
The flute's "sweet, soft, wailing harmonies," he says, "soften a
man's spirit as iron is softened," and make it "useful from having
been useless and hard" (411a), but the flute and the wailing
harmonies are banned from the city (399d). Just as the guardians'
different treatment of familiars and strangers does not mean that
they are philosophic as well as spirited, their education in music
does not nurture a balanced soul. The city of guardians differs
from the city of simple artisans out of which it grew not because
its leading men are more complex, with desires that lead to
change, but because their simplicity is not natural. Their simplicity must be imposed through education and institutional
arrangements.

By obscuring the hardening effect of the city's music, Socrates is hiding the hardness of the guardians' souls and the city's
suppression of the soul's gentler elements. The guardians have
not become gentle men who moderate their actions out of a
concern for those among whom they live. They are hard men
who derive their sense of identity solely from their city and who
therefore fight passionately to preserve it whatever the cost.
Aristotle observed that Socrates made the guardians fiercer than
they ought to be (*Politics*, 1328a8–12). He made them, in fact,
all spiritedness. Conforming to the city's requirements, they are
cruel to themselves, abrogating any personal identity that distinguishes them from others and from the city itself. In the name
of their city, they destroy whatever is peculiarly their own.

Despite the absolute security spiritedness tries to produce
for the city, Socrates suggests that it should be moderated by
gentleness and philosophy. Spiritedness can evidently go too far
in its harsh maintenance of unity. But gentleness and philosophy
become distorted in the guardians. Gentleness to others is transformed into an identification with the whole city, and philosophy

is limited to defending the known or the familiar. What Socrates presents as a means of moderating the harshness of the city only reinforces it. The "most manly" Glaucon finds this acceptable, just as he has no complaints about the city's communism.

The Tripartite Soul

After Socrates describes the guardians' education and way of life, he searches for justice in the city as a prelude to finding it in the soul. He claims that justice is each class in the city—or each part of the soul—doing its own job. Both city and soul have three parts: guardian rulers in the city correspond to reason in the soul, guardian soldiers to spiritedness, and the artisans and farmers to desire. By comparing the soldiers in the city with spiritedness in the soul, Socrates silently drops the fiction that their natures balance spiritedness with philosophy, or hard elements with soft ones. If the soldiers' harshness is moderated at all, it is due to their alliance with the rulers rather than to any gentleness within their own souls. But that alliance is for the sake of controlling the city's farmers and artisans, just as spiritedness is allied with reason in the soul for the sake of controlling desire. This job of the soldiers, and this function of spiritedness, can very well necessitate cruelty to one's own. Cruelty, if requisite to the performance of the job, would be nothing other than justice.

In order to show that the soul has distinct parts, Socrates supposes the case of a man who is both thirsty and unwilling to drink. There must be something in his soul bidding him to drink and something forbidding him to do so. What forbids proceeds from calculation, Socrates says, while what draws is due to affections and diseases (439c–d). But why is this result necessary? A man might calculate the propriety of going forward, and a state of disease might cause him to hold back. Socrates ignores this possibility, implying that all "longing to take something" and "embracing" are unhealthy, and all "rejecting" and "thrusting away" are reasonable. In this way, he arrives at the existence

of two parts of the soul: the calculating and the irrational, or
"the part with which it loves, hungers, thirsts, and is agitated
by the other desires" (439d). All desires and loves are irrational,
and it is the job of the calculating part of the soul to hold them
down. "Longing to take something" and "embracing," which
this account depreciates as irrational, indicate the neediness of
an incomplete or imperfect soul aware of its own insufficiency.
"Rejecting" and "thrusting away," on the other hand, suggest
sufficiency: a man does not need what he rejects. The conflict
in the soul Socrates is describing thus indicates man's fight
against incompleteness in an attempt to be self-sufficient.[3] The
suppression of desire, however, prevents a man from pursuing
the good things that he lacks; it forecloses change and growth.
Although Socrates originally referred to this highest part of
the soul as that by which we learn (436a), he now presents its primary function as ruling the irrational elements in the soul.[4] In
the discussion of the spirited guardian, philosophy appeared
as a defense of the familiar rather than as an inquiry into the
unknown. Similarly, in the soul that parallels the city, reason
maintains a proper internal structure rather than learning something new.

Socrates illustrates the operation of the third part of the
soul—"the part that contains spirit and with which we are spirited—with the story of Leontius (439e). When Leontius is over-
powered by his desire to look at corpses left by the public
executioner, he is disgusted with himself and angry at his desire.
This disgust and anger, according to Socrates, is a sign of his
spiritedness. Socrates does not explain why Leontius wants to
look at the corpses or why he struggles against his desire. The
sight of death conveys a sense of impermanence, an understanding that can justify inactivity and support human weakness. Spiritedness rebels at such weakness, just as it fights in general against
desire, which reveals incompleteness or insufficiency. This is
true of the desire for food and drink, which Socrates mentioned
when he first spoke of the desiring part of the soul (439d), but
also of the desire to look upon human mortality.

The particular corpses that Leontius wants to see, reveal

that men come into conflict with their city. Here the conflict is
so great that men are publicly executed. By trying to prevent
Leontius from looking at the corpses, spiritedness attempts to
hide the disjunction between the individual and the city. Spiritedness rebels not only against death but also against the truth
that man needs something for his satisfaction that goes beyond
his city, beyond what he can create and control. On different
levels, spiritedness denies man's vulnerability. This is why its
most common manifestation is anger at insult. Spiritedness
makes a man stand up for himself, proud and strong, refusing
to be scorned, used, or even affected by another. Spiritedness
seeks absolute control.

Like Leontius' spiritedness, the city Socrates describes tries
to hide any necessary disjunction between the individual and the
community. The guardians must totally identify with the city;
and they are supposed to be complete through this identification,
for they have no private pleasures or unsatisfied desires. The
spirited city, which takes unity as its goal (462a–b), tries to
minimize man's vulnerability and even to make him invulnerable. Spiritedness underlies politics, for through politics men
seek to order or control their affairs so that their existence is
stable and secure. Suppressing desires that lead men to embrace
what is alien and warding off novelty and change might be
necessary for such security. The spiritedness underlying politics
insists on coherence and even simplicity. It tries to make men
believe that they have only one art by nature. Men will use force
in order to maintain their political arrangements. Socrates indicates that spiritedness is potentially violent. He even imagines
that it operates in beasts (441b, cf. Aristotle, *Nicomachean Ethics*,
1116b31–32). Leontius' spiritedness would, if it could, root out
his desire to look at the corpses. His spiritedness strikes at his
eyes as "damned wretches" who will look no matter what
(440a).

Despite the violence of spiritedness, Socrates associates its
action with reason: spiritedness turns against desires, he says,
"when desires force someone contrary to the calculating part [of
his soul]" (440b). But it is not clear from Socrates' account,

whether reason or spiritedness has the upper hand in their alliance. If spiritedness is man's drive to make himself invulnerable, it can account for reason's calculation against desire, which reveals man's dependence or incompleteness. In Socrates' example of reason's struggle against desire, reason fights to preserve a man from being harmed. And when Socrates illustrates spiritedness' fight against desire with the story of Leontius, he is completely silent about the role of reason. Spiritedness obviously has a force of its own. A man unable to accept his vulnerability would prefer to view philosophy as a defender of the familiar rather than as an avenue into perplexing questions, just as he would designate the soul's highest function as maintaining order rather than pursuing the truth. Socrates' discussion of man's situation in the *Republic* is colored by the spirited drives of his interlocutors, just as Plato's portrayal of that discussion is meant to reveal the nature and limits of spiritedness. Reason no more rules spiritedness in the soul Socrates describes than gentleness moderates spiritedness in the education of the guardians. There is a similar problem in Socrates' description of the city's philosophers. They are nominally the city's rulers, but it is the city that educates them and compels them to rule. There is reason to believe that the *Republic* describes a politicization of philosophy rather than an elevation of politics to a philosophic level.

Socrates defines the virtues in the tripartite soul so that they parallel those in the city. Justice in the city is each man's doing his own job or minding his own business. Similarly, "the three classes in [the] soul [of the just man do not] meddle with each other," but each performs its own job (443d). The just man's excellence depends on nothing outside but consists in the perfect working of his parts. Justice exists, Socrates says, "not with respect to a man's minding his external business, but with respect to what is within, with respect to what truly concerns him and his own" (443d). The just man thus embodies the initial conception of spiritedness: his concern is completely for his own. If he does not seem to ward off the alien, it is because he does not come into contact with it. He "harmonizes the three parts [of his soul] just like the three notes on a harmonic scale, lowest, highest, and middle" (443d). In the just man, spiritedness appears to maintain an internal harmony uninfluenced by anything outside. He is self-sufficient—his self-contained goodness is dependent on no one. He is not essentially involved in anything external, whether actions in which his justice becomes manifest or relationships with others that are characterized by justice. Defined solely by his internal harmony and without actions and relationships of his own, he differs in no way from any other just man. He is an idea rather than a human being. He has no more individual identity than the guardians. Man's spirited drive toward self-sufficiency leads this conception of justice; it is a justice divorced from any consequences, self-contained and unchanging. It answers Glaucon's demand for something simply good, a demand answered more completely by the ideas the city's philosophers contemplate.[5] These ideas are simple and unchanging; they possess the complete invulnerability the spirited man craves. The city's philosophers are less philosophic than spirited. In them, philosophy is distorted to serve the city.

Spirited Philosophy

Socrates introduces philosophy as an explicit theme in the *Republic* when he claims that the city must have philosophic rulers in order to come into being. Philosophy thus appears not as the way of life proper to man, valuable for its own sake, but as an instrument of the city. This application of philosophy is implicit throughout Socrates' treatment of philosophy in the *Republic*.

Since philosophy means literally "love of wisdom," Socrates explains its meaning by first defining love. When a man loves something, Socrates says, "he desires all of that class," rather than "one part of it and not another." Socrates' account of love is odd, for it assumes that lovers have no preferences.

Why does Socrates present such an inaccurate view of love? In the first place, the man who lives under communism must love in the way Socrates describes: only if he loves all the members of a class—all the other guardians—will the "community of pleasures and pains" exist (464a). Should a guardian have a preference for one woman over another, for example, he would be dissatisfied with marriage arrangements that did not take his preference into account. More important, however, if a man loves all the members of a class, there is less risk that he lose his beloved. The guardian will lose the object of his love completely only if the city itself is destroyed. Because he loves no one in particular, he cannot suffer from the contingencies that plague lovers. Communism of women and children, like the public tales, thus aims at overcoming the pain of death. It is animated by spiritedness. Socrates' account of love reveals more about spiritedness than eros.[6]

Socrates then considers philosophers, who love all of wisdom and are "willing to taste every kind of learning with gusto" (475d). This implies, according to Glaucon, that "many strange ones" are to be counted among the philosophers, such as "lovers of sights" and "lovers of hearing," who although they are unwilling to attend a discussion "run around to every chorus at the Dionysia, just as though they had hired out their ears for hearing" (475d). Glaucon disdains these lovers of the pleasures of the senses, among whom he includes men who take pleasure in tragedy. He himself obviously dislikes tragedy and does not run to every chorus at the Dionysia. Tragedy reveals men's weakness, their inability to control their situation, and their vulnerability.

Socrates relieves Glaucon's disappointment by refining his conception of the lover of wisdom. The lovers of sensation and "delight in beautiful sounds and colors and shapes and all that craft makes from such things," while the philosopher delights "in the nature of the beautiful itself." It is not all learning that the philosopher loves, but the universal characteristic that all the particular things that appear to the senses have in common. Socrates has changed the object of love from all the members of a class to the class itself. He is not contradicting his first statement about love, however; he is explaining it. If a man loves all the members of a class, he loves them because they embody some characteristic they have in common rather than because of characteristics peculiar to each member. When a guardian loves all the other guardians, he is loving the embodiments of a class characteristic rather than particular human beings. His love is a reflection of the love Socrates attributes to the philosopher, who loves class characteristics or ideas. The philosopher runs even less risk with the object of his love: members of classes perish, classes do not. These "lovers of wisdom" who will rule the city live so as to minimize, if not eliminate, their vulnerability. Unlike Leontius, they succeed in averting their gaze from the transcience of human life.

In clarifying what the philosopher loves, Socrates distinguishes knowledge, opinion, and ignorance and their respective objects. He says that a man knows what is but is ignorant of what is not. And opinions, which fall between knowledge and ignorance, have as their object what falls between existing and not existing—everything that comes into being and passes away—the world we know through our senses. These objects that cannot be fully known are merely those that delight lovers of sight and hearing, or the many beautiful things, for example, that, falling short of beauty itself, partake of its opposite as well— if they are not simply beautiful, they are also ugly (479a–b). This account of what philosophers love trivializes complex and changing objects and the opinions men form of them. But this includes human beings themselves and the understandings they have of themselves and their lives—the very objects of Socrates' own political philosophy. Unlike Socrates, whose search for knowledge never ends, philosophers who rule the city find a world of ideas that is absolutely certain and secure. They are surprisingly apolitical.[7]

Socrates indicates the problem in turning the city over to these philosophers when he admits that to one who "contemplates all time and being," "human life [does not seem] anything great" (486a). Are those who do not consider human life very great, however, the best ones to provide for human life by ruling the city? Is their vision of "what is always the same in all respects" (484b) useful for managing a city, where one finds complex and changing affairs? Socrates' description of how the city's philos-

ophers put the eternal things they contemplate "into the dispositions of men" (500d) gives more cause for alarm: they "take
the city and the dispositions of human beings, as though they
were a tablet, which, in the first place, they would wipe clean"
(501a). Lovers of only eternal objects, they have no compunc-
tions about erasing the ordinary activities of human life.

Socrates confirms the dangers of rule by philosophers when
he indicates the incompleteness of human knowledge. Speaking
of the good, the "greatest study" of philosophers (505a), he says
"the soul divines that it is something but is at a loss about it and
unable to get a sufficient grasp of what it is" (505d–e). The soul's
divination of the good suggests that opinion has a higher status
than its previous depreciation led us to expect. Because what
men divine of the good is reflected in their opinions, their opinions are intelligible. Indeed, Socrates' constant exploration and
correction of opinions implies their intelligibility. But because
men have an insufficient grasp of the good, Socrates does not
try to rule in the manner of philosopher-kings. Referring to the
good, Socrates says, "those best men in the city into whose
hands we put everything [should not be] in the dark about a
thing of this kind and importance" (506a).

As Socrates continues his account of the philosopher-kings,
however, the incompleteness of human knowledge is forgotten.
Through a mathematical education, they ascend from becoming
to being. In order to show how mathematics is the key to such
an education, Socrates explains that sensation is defective because
it "doesn't reveal one thing more than its opposite" (523c). Any
perceived object, for example, is larger than some objects but
smaller than others, or harder than some objects but softer than
others. Man's intellect must determine that largeness and smallness are two separate things. It must "[do] the opposite of what
sight did" (524d), for sight presented largeness and smallness as
existing together in the same object, insofar as the object is
compared to other objects both larger and smaller than itself.
The intellect is to move from the sensed world of relationships
to simple things that are what they are without coming into
relation to anything outside themselves. The intellect that Soc-

rates describes does not so much build upon sense, moving from hard objects to hardness itself, as it denies the evidence of the senses, moving from complexity to simplicity. The number that Socrates proposes as the key to the philosophers' education is the prime illustration of how man abstracts from the evidence of the senses. For sensation, "nothing looks as if it were one more than the opposite of one" (524e). "We see the same thing," Socrates says, "at the same time as both one and as unlimited multitude" (525a). That is, each thing looks as if it were one thing and also as if it possessed many opposite qualities, such as largeness and smallness or hardness and softness. The study of number aims at discovering an indivisible one that is not composed of an infinite multitude. Number and calculation should not be taken up as they are now, Socrates concludes, for mathematicians discuss "numbers that are attached to visible or tangible bodies" (525d). Philosopher-kings, in contrast, seek a one "equal to every other one, without the slightest difference between them." (526a).

The unity sought by the philosopher-kings' mathematics abstracts from all the differences among the things counted. This mathematics is the fitting preparation for philosophers who are to introduce communism in the city.[8] The simple men in the city, for whom there is no privacy, are each "equal to every other one, without the slightest difference between them, and containing no parts within [themselves]." The politics of the *Republic*'s city, like the philosophers' mathematical education, finds no limits in "visible or tangible bodies," whose particular identities constitute limits to the city's absolute unity.

The other mathematical studies in the philosophers' education are all supposed to have the same effect—turning philosophers away from becoming toward being, until they are able to grasp the good itself (532d). Dialectic, which usually refers to the conversations between Socrates and particular interlocutors as they explore the numerous sides or facets of a phenomenon, is included among these mathematical studies. This dialectic, however, does not appear to involve shared speech, for through it the philosophers attain the being of each thing "by means of argument without the use of any of the senses" (532a). Their dialectic is inaudible, private, and not limited like a Socratic conversation by the presence of an interlocutor.[9]

The spiritedness that defends the familiar might seem opposed to the city's philosophers whose mathematical education moves them from becoming to being. But the greatest threat to the self, which spiritedness tries to preserve against change and death, is the familiar world of becoming. The philosophers renounce that world for one of simple beings, for simple beings are least vulnerable to change (380d). The philosophy that escapes from the world of change is as spirited as the guardian's education and the soul that suppresses desire. That philosophy is the repudiation of Socratic philosophizing, which explores the familiar world that philosopher-kings escape, and which investigates human affairs rather than "the things in the heavens" (cf. 516a–b and *Apology*, 19b–d). Insofar as philosophy is best illustrated by Socrates' life, the city's distortion of philosophy to serve its needs is a destruction of philosophy.

Spiritedness underlies the philosophizing of the city's rulers, and it also characterizes their rule. After dialectic leads them to the good, they "use it as a pattern for ordering the city, private men, and themselves" (540b). By instituting communism in the city and by depicting models of self-sufficiency in the public tales, the rulers go further than merely using the good as a pattern for ordering the complex affairs and human beings in the city. They try to endow what they find in the city with the simplicity of their model. But to impose simplicity on complexity is to destroy complexity. The rule of these mathematically trained philosophers will destroy the city. Socrates intimates the destructiveness fostered by the philosophers' mathematical studies, for he describes them as useful for making war as well as for contemplating being (522c–d, 525b–c, 527c).

Socrates concludes his discussion of the genesis of the city by describing how it is founded by true philosophers: "All those in the city who happen to be older than ten they will send out to the country; and taking over their children they will rear them—far away from those dispositions they now have from their parents—in their own manners and laws that are such as we described before" (540e–541a). The adults who have families and private concerns and who will resist assimilation into an undifferentiated unity must be removed. Socrates does not mention how parents "sent out to the country" and deprived of their children will react. He speaks of exile, although the situation calls for mass murder. Only the children, the unformed members of the city, can be allowed to live, for they can be molded by the new education.

In its destruction of the adult population of the city, the spirited drive for absolute certainty and control ends in perfect horror. The actual destruction of human beings, however, is the logical outcome of the disregard for the individual identities of men manifest in the guardians' education and the institution of communism. Because spiritedness will admit no limits to the unity it seeks, it destroys both cities, which are necessarily made up of parts, and philosophy, which contemplates the variety of phenomena that compose the cosmos.

In the *Republic*, Socrates describes a political situation in which harsh or spirited elements predominate over gentle ones. Spiritedness gives order or coherence to the human world by imposing unity on the diverse elements in the soul and the city and by limiting man's various possibilities. Although this task of spiritedness is necessary for human life, it also holds the potential for tyranny, for the unity that affords complete security destroys the parts of the city and the complexity of the soul. The *Republic* presents this potential in its description of the communistic city and its philosophy. If spiritedness realizes this potential, human life becomes sterile, and spiritedness consumes itself, for it has nothing left worth defending.

The justice that Socrates describes is the simple order imposed on life by spiritedness and ultimately the idea contemplated by philosopher-kings. Is there no justice, however, that reflects the complexity of the soul and of city and is able to guide men as they come into contact with changing situations and different human beings? It is in Socrates' actions in the Platonic dialogues rather than in the city in speech and its cosmology that such a justice can be found. Far from treating his interlocutors as members of a class, Socrates speaks to each as his particular character warrants. At the same time, he attends to the complexity of whatever he discusses, and allows the tensions or contradictions to emerge. Through understanding these tensions and contradictions men can moderate their drive for absolute unity or perfection, for a pure justice unmixed with its opposite and divorced from any consequences. Socratic political philosophy thus makes spiritedness gentle. Socrates offers guidance and direction by controlling the discussion and ordering priorities. But the order of his conversations is anchored in the individual natures of his interlocutors and the complexity of the phenomena. The community that he forms with others is a model for a limited rule that constitutes an alternative to the communistic city of the *Republic*.

Notes

1. I have used the translation by Allan Bloom, *The Republic of Plato with Notes and an Interpretive Essay* (New York: Basic Books, 1968). Small parts of the argument of this essay have previously been published in my *Socrates and the Political Community: An Ancient Debate* (Albany, N.Y.: SUNY Press, 1987), and "The *Republic*'s Two Alternatives: Philosopher-Kings and Socrates," *Political Theory*, vol. 12, no. 2 (May 1984), 252–74.

2. Many commentators find nothing surprising in Socrates' designation of the dog as philosophic. Ernest Barker, for example, explains the rationality of the dog's actions: "by the use of the faculty of knowledge (which is reason), it distinguishes between friend and foe," *The Political Thought of Plato and Aristotle* (New York: Dover Publications, 1959), p. 109. See also Richard Lewis Nettleship, *Lectures on the Republic of Plato* (London: Macmillan, 1901) p. 75. Bloom, in contrast, notes that Socrates' comparison of philosophers to dogs is "not serious." But he finds it justified in the limited sense that the warriors' "love of the known extends their affections beyond themselves to the city; it partakes of the universalizing or cosmopolitan effect of philosophy" ("Interpretive Essay," p. 351).

I argue, however, that it is not because the guardians are open that the comparison between them and philosophy is apt, but because the philosophers who rule the city are closed. The comparison may be more serious than it first appears.

3. Two related errors might prevent one from seeing the full extent of the depreciation of desire and the denial of incompleteness that occurs in this soul that parallels the city. In the first place, one might interpret the desires that Socrates presents as hostile to reason merely as physical ones. Although Socrates gives hunger and thirst as examples of desire, however, in the discussion of spiritedness, the desire at issue is a desire to look at corpses. In the second place, one might erroneously attribute love or desire to the calculating part of the soul Socrates is describing here. See note below.

4. Commentators typically attribute both functions, learning and ruling, to the rational part of the soul without seeing that the latter replaces the former in Socrates' account in Book IV. See, for example, Barker, *The Political Thought of Plato and Aristotle*, p. 104, and Nettleship, *Lectures on the Republic of Plato*, p. 157. Julia Annas does observe that of reason's two roles—to rule in the soul and "to love and search for the truth in all its manifestations"—the second is "not much stressed in Book IV" (*An Introduction to Plato's Republic* [Oxford: Oxford University Press, 1981], p. 134). She does not, however, explain why this is the case.

5. For an analysis of Glaucon's character and his role in the *Republic*, see my "Glaucon's Adaptation of the Story of Gyges and its Implications for Plato's Political Teaching," *Polity*, vol. XVII, no. 1 (Fall 1984), 30–39.

6. Commentators usually assume that Socrates is presenting his own understanding of love here and do not note anything untrue about it. See, for example, James Adam, *The Republic of Plato* (Cambridge: Cambridge University Press, 1969), vol. I, note on line 474d23, p. 333, and Paul Friedlander, *Plato: The Dialogues, Second and Third Periods*, trans. Hans Meyerhoff (Princeton: Princeton University Press, 1969), p. 106.

7. For a further contrast between Socrates and the *Republic*'s philosopher-kings, see my "The *Republic*'s Two Alternatives." Bloom presents a different interpretation of Socrates' relation to the city in the *Republic*. He argues that Socrates is constructing a regime that is especially suited to him—"one in which philosophy does not have to be a private, hidden activity because it contradicts the

authoritative prejudices" ("Interpretive Essay," p. 387). But it is not clear to me that the city in speech has any room for Socrates. For example, it has its own set of authoritative prejudices, such as the one-man, one-art formula, to say nothing of the noble lie. Although the city's rulers may understand that the noble lie is a lie salutary for the city and that the members of the city are not descended from the same mother, do they understand that its teaching about homogeneity and simplicity is untrue? This is a teaching, I would argue, that their mathematical education makes them inclined to accept.

8. Commentators typically believe that Socrates' presentation of the philosopher-kings' education is, in the words of H. B. Joseph, "what Plato thought that a philosophic—i.e., the highest—education should be," (*Knowledge and the Good in Plato's Republic*, reprint of the 1948 Oxford University Press edition [Westport, Connecticut: Greenwood Press, 1981], p. 1). John Burnet suggests that Socrates here gives the curriculum of the Academy itself (*Platonism* [Berkeley: The University of California Press, 1928], pp. 101–02).

9. Annas tries to assimilate the Socratic conversation to the study included in the philosopher-kings' education. She is not deterred by the fact that the two understandings of dialectic "at first glance do not happily go together" (*An Introduction to Plato's Republic*, p. 282).

ANN P.
CHARNEY

IV

Spiritedness and Piety
in Aristotle

In the *Nicomachean Ethics*, Aristotle begins his consideration of the political role and meaning of spiritedness with a critique of the Homeric heroes. He questions both the identification of the Homeric hero's spiritedness with courage and the piety of the hero's conception of the gods. Through Aristotle's analysis of the qualities mistaken for courage, the Homeric hero is shown to be moved by spiritedness stemming from fear of the bad opinion of others, and his piety is shown to be a hope for the favorable opinion of the gods. This spiritedness and this piety turn out to be the opposite sides of the same coin: the desire for immortality. Aristotle replaces Homeric courage with true courage derived from one's own reason (the highest manifestation of which is philosophy), but he is silent about the nature of true piety. Instead, he advocates an earthly justice, which prevents injustice and promotes mutual assistance, and the self-sufficiency that comes through contemplation or philosophy. Spiritedness and piety converge in the imitation of the gods. This convergence illuminates the relation between one's own and the good. Rational self-love and a just concern for others coalesce in the magnanimous man who through spiritedness joins the parts of the city in friendship. The magnanimous man also brings the city and the philosopher together by educating the city in the noble or the beautiful. The activity of the magnanimous man is the physical and human reflection of immortality. To maintain both the good of the individual and the well-being of the city is the essence of spiritedness. To dedicate oneself to sustaining such a balance deserves the title of true piety.

Spiritedness, Piety, and the Homeric Hero

Aristotle's judgment on spiritedness is indicated in his first extended discussion of the moral virtues, where he relegates spiritedness to the third remove from the virtue of courage.[1] Courage is a mean between fear and confidence. An excess of fearlessness has no name but could be called madness or insensitivity to pain; an excess of confidence in the face of fearful things is rashness; excessive fear is cowardice, as is defective confidence. Although others might be called courageous metaphorically, the courageous man, unfrightened, faces death in battle where there are dangers against which one can defend oneself or die nobly. Spiritedness is ranked among the five illusory types of courage. The first type has two aspects: political courage attaches, on the one hand, to citizens who face death for the sake of honors or for evading penalties or shame. On the other hand, it attaches to troops who fear the certain pain that will be inflicted on them by their generals if they do not fight—a compulsory political courage. The apparent courage of seasoned troops whose experience tells them they are in no danger is second, followed by spiritedness. Fourth is the courage of the sanguine, who have an unfounded confidence in their own powers. The apparent courage of the sanguine is parallel to the fifth type, the courage of the ignorant, who face danger without realizing the gravity of the situation. The sanguine and the ignorant have an unfounded confidence in their surroundings.

For Aristotle, then, spiritedness is different from courage. Courage is deliberate and, fully aware of the dangers, stands firm; spiritedness is impetuous, driven it would seem by fear or pain. When driven by pain, spiritedness seeks revenge or a desperate salvation. As wild beasts are emboldened by pain, so spirited men rush blindly into dangerous situations. Such a blind attack cannot be called courageous, says Aristotle, any more than can the hunger of the asses who attack the wheatfields oblivious to cudgels or the daring of the lustful adulterer.[2] Rather than a fixed disposition to face nobly the dangers of war and death, spiritedness in this sense is a brutish response to pain. Aristotle's example of the wounded animal emphasizes the irrational aspect of spiritedness (cf. 1147a11–20). Despite this Aristotle says that the courageous man is essentially spirited (*thymoeidēs*), adding to natural spiritedness reason, purpose, and choice and action for the sake of the noble. Nevertheless, whatever the nature of spiritedness may be, it is in itself not the moral virtue of courage.

It is not only spiritedness that is demoted in the section on courage, but also those spirited men who were considered to be courage incarnate, the Homeric heroes. Homer is not quoted in those passages where Aristotle speaks of true courage but only in the passages on political courage and spiritedness. His heroes serve as examples in Aristotle's remarks on both kinds of political courage. The first quotation presents Hector's fear of shame: "Polydamas will be the first to flout me" (*Iliad* XXII.100). Hector, well aware of the inferiority of his strength to Achilles', refuses to hide from Achilles for fear that Polydamas will blame him, for his earlier Zeus-abetted overconfidence that caused the Trojans to overextend themselves. Despite the fact that his sense of shame further endangers the Trojans, he resolves to fight Achilles in order to know "which one the Olympians will give glory to"—a surprising reason, given Achilles' manifest physical superiority.[3]

Aristotle next cites a passage quoting Diomedes that has much to do with Hector: "Hector will make his boast at Troy hereafter, 'By me was Tydeus' son' " (*Iliad* VIII.148). Diomedes bravely attempted to rescue old, courageous Nestor from Hector. He is so successful that he almost kills Hector. This arouses Zeus, who dotes on Hector, to throw a lightning bolt to scare off Diomedes. He convinces Nestor to retreat, but Diomedes is afraid Hector will boast of his victory. It takes three more lightning bolts to persuade Diomedes, partly because Hector is indeed taunting him. Hector and the Trojans take heart from Zeus' signs, and the Achaeans would have been routed had not Zeus

at the last minute sent a sign to renew their hope. Both passages
that Aristotle cites concern occasions when the sense of shame
or fear of blame causes the heroes to act contrary to good military
strategy. We see Hector both jeering and fearing jeers: the
Homeric heroes can use this weapon because they are so vulnerable to it.

In the section on compulsory political courage, Aristotle,
after quoting Hector and Diomedes correctly, ascribes to Hector
a threat made by Agamemnon: "Whomsoever I see cowering
far from the battle, He will be certain not to escape the dogs"
(1116a34). This is a studied error on Aristotle's part intended to
show the connection between the two kinds of political courage.[4]
In addition, Aristotle changes the Homeric passage. The original
reads: "Whomsoever I see tarry by the curved ships *willingly* far
from the battle, He then will be certain not to escape the dogs
and birds" (*Iliad* II.391, italics mine).[5] In compulsory political
courage, the commanders make the fear of battle secondary to
fear of the certain death they will inflict on cowards. Aristotle
removes the word *willingly* from the Homeric passage, because
neither the courage nor the cowardice of political courage is
voluntarily chosen, and he substitutes the word "cowering." He
indicates that even the bravest acts of political courage are a form
of cowardice, a blind, unreasoning flight from pain.[6] But since
shame is also a kind of pain (as are civil penalties), the first kind
of political courage is also the result of the fear of pain, its actions
as little reasoned as—albeit more noble than—the actions of compulsory political courage.[7]

The wish to avoid civil penalties or military firing squads
is prudent, as is the fear of shame, if such a consideration is the
result of a reasoned assessment of its correctness. As the Homeric
allusions show, however, Aristotle objects to political courage
because of its dogmatic, dog-like qualities. Just as dogs bark at
all strangers, so political courage avoids all punishments no matter what the consequences, and it fears all adverse opinion no
matter how ill-informed or ill-willed. Moreover, the slightest
omen encourages Homeric heroes beyond reason or discourages
them beyond ingenuity. The defective character of the political

courage that stands in awe of the opinions of others is under-
scored at the end of Book IV, where Aristotle asserts that awe
is not a virtue.[8] Aristotle attributes Agamemnon's threat to Hector in order to indicate the connection between these two kinds
of political courage. The common thread is the lack of reason
informing any of the actions. Hector is also used because he is
susceptible to the inducements of political courage and because
he of all the heroes is most harmed by his dependence on omens
and opinions.

These characteristics of political courage are close to Aristotle's conception of spiritedness as rooted in fear or pain or
certain desires. In part, this is why Homeric passages appear also
in Aristotle's discussion of spiritedness. Two of these passages
refer to the spiritedness imparted to the combatants by the gods
in the *Iliad*.[9] Spiritedness engendered by a belief in the arbitrary,
vengeful Homeric gods does not elicit the knowledge and reasoning requisite to true courage. This belief is based on an unreasoning hope for physical participation in the eternal. And
behind that desire for immortality lies a greater fear for the
destruction of the body than of the soul. As political courage is
the capitulation to man's passions, so spiritedness is the appease-
ment of the passions of the gods. Aristotle blames the Homeric
heroes for failure to attend properly to the soul. Though Hector
is pained by the blame of Polydamus, he does not learn from
the pain how to avoid bringing new harm upon his city. His
mistake in facing Achilles, thus leaving Troy leaderless, is a
mistake he has made before: he allows his trust in omens to cloud
his rational powers of assessment. He is not courageous enough
to be afraid. Diomedes' fear of obloquy also has a physical root.
Diomedes dreads the opinion of his enemies, not of his fellow
citizens. His shame is based on the fear of what others can do
to the weak. His self-assessment comes to depend on the assessment of others, his purpose to influence that assessment. His
soul is enslaved to others.

What, then, is courage? Courage is a mean between the
extremes of fear and confidence, Aristotle says. The vices attached to courage, though, are excesses of these extremes: cour-

age is the only moral virtue the extremes of which themselves
have extremes and are therefore not simply bad. The vice con-
current with courage is not confidence: it is an excess or defect
of confidence. Thus, there can be an appropriate amount of fear
on certain occasions. One of these occasions could be facing
death; Aristotle would then be calling into question the citizen's
duty to defend the city. But Aristotle says that the courageous
man is without terror when facing a noble death, and that the
noblest death is in battle. Though it is courageous to fear some
things, it is not courageous to fear armed combat. Moreover,
the courageous man is also without terror (but not without pain
[1117b10–16]) when facing such dangers as death at sea, where
defending oneself or dying nobly is not possible. Though death
is the "most fearful thing," the courageous man does not
fear it.

　　Aristotle's examination of the moral virtues, beginning
with courage, is prefaced by a discussion of voluntary actions
or the possibility of human freedom. Courage differs from spiritedness in that courage includes reason as well as passion, despite
the fact that courage is a virtue of the irrational part of the soul.
Reason, not spiritedness, is the touchstone of courage. But courage from the perspective of reason looks quite different from
political courage. Courage is concerned with facing death nobly;
but it also includes the strength to flee death when it is fitting
to do so. It is the ability to judge dispassionately, free from
opinion or shame, the right time, reason, and manner of enduring or fearing the right things (1115b20). If one ought not
to fear anything not due to oneself, and if death is yet fearful,
then the courageous man judges the occasion for facing death
using standards supplied by reason. The courageous man might
well avoid a battle in order to win the war. Certainly he would
not be impetuous but would be "slow to act, and only in the
great and notable deeds" (1124b25). Courage must be accompanied by knowledge—which is not the same as saying that
courage is knowledge.[10]

　　The occasions for fear are "above the human" (1115b8),
things feared by everyone with intelligence. These are the oc-

casions for the courage that fears to the appropriate degree—that is neither excessive nor deficient in fearing, both of which show a lack of intellect. These above human things are the divine. It is possible "to fear such things too much and too little; and also to fear things that are not fearful as if they were fearful" (1115b14). Fearing the divine too much results in paralysis because of the vastness of the unknown. The belief that they are loved by the gods causes the rash spiritedness of the Homeric heroes: they feared such things too little. Believing that the gods are evil or ill-willed toward humans is to fear things not fearful. The proper attitude, an appropriate amount of fear,[11] is best depicted in Aristotle's description of courage. Aristotle restores or reconstitutes spiritedness when he declares both that a courage stemming from spiritedness seems most natural, and that when spiritedness is combined with rational choice and a view of the end, it really is courage. Spiritedness combined with intellect is needed to philosophize in the face of the knowledge of one's ignorance about the gods. The philosopher, however, pursues the truth as the ass his grain or the adulterer his beloved, a sign that the truth is pleasant. One kind of spiritedness is kindled by desire.

Piety, Spiritedness, and the Aristotelian City

Fearing the gods in the appropriate manner seems to be the definition of piety. Piety, manifesting itself as philosophy, is no longer fitting or needed to support the courage to face death in battle. Does any place remain for piety in the political domain? There is, in all of Aristotle's discussions of virtue, no virtue of Piety. In keeping with this omission, there is little mention of the gods or the requirements of religion in other areas where they might be expected. Advice on the religious arrangements of the city in the *Politics* is minimal. Religious magistrates are brought into Aristotle's discussion of the magistracy in Book VI, but not in his more prominent discussion of it in Book IV. In his consideration of the parts necessary to the "regime according to prayer" in Book VII, Aristotle lists the priests in his first enumeration but omits them in his summary count. Even when he remarks on the need for officers to order the city's religious observances, he makes no mention of the form or content of these religious arrangements, still less connecting them with the ends of the city.[12]

One would also expect reference to the gods in the context of justice and the laws in view of Aristotle's association with Plato. The inquiry into justice in Plato's *Republic* ends with, and seems to depend on, the theological myth of Book X. In the *Laws*, the laws endure not because they are just but because the citizens are pious. Plato's Socrates does not neglect considerations of piety in relation to the justice of the individual or to stability and excellence in the community. In Aristotle's account of justice (*Nicomachean Ethics*, Book V), in contrast, the only named divinities are the Graces (*Charitēs*), goddesses of joy, natural beauty, and bodily grace. The Graces are presented as a symbol or reminder of requital in a prelude to the discussion of corrective justice in the exchange of goods. Association for exchange is not possible without proportional reciprocity. The city, too, requires proportionate requital to remain together: if men cannot requite evil for evil, they think themselves slaves; if they cannot do good for good, there is no sharing, without which the city cannot long endure. "This is why they put a shrine of the Graces in a public place [literally, "at our feet"], so that there be a repayment. For this is peculiar to grace: one must not only return a service in gratitude, but another time initiate the favor" (1133a2). Though the Graces are divine, their purpose is not to remind us of the gods but to recall our duties to our fellow men.

Aristotle refers to religious matters again in Book V, in his discussion of political justice. Political justice or right has two parts, the natural and the conventional. The just by nature concerns the unchangeable things ("the natural has everywhere the same force" [1134b20]); conventional right derives its force from its decree. Aristotle's refusal to give examples of natural right has been the source of difficulty and controversy. The examples of conventionally just actions, however, point to the general dictates of natural right. Among the examples of the conventional are "to sacrifice one goat, and not two sheep; and such special legislation as sacrificing to Brasidas" (1134b18–24). When Aristotle speaks of sacrifice in general, he looks not at the gods to whom one sacrifices, nor to the reason for sacrificing, but at the objects to be sacrificed. When he considers the recipient of a sacrifice, he looks at a particular human being, Brasidas, the Spartan general.

The omission of the gods and the mention of a contemporary war hero carry through the perspective in Aristotle's discussion of courage. In Homer the gods bestow immortal glory on the heroes; in the *Ethics* the bestowal of glory is a part of the city's justice that is connected to natural right.[13] Though the honors given by Amphipolis occur after Brasidas' death, it is important that the city memorialize him. Gratitude is needed to indicate to potential defenders that the city will reward them in return for their deeds. The treachery toward Athens by Alcibiades (who is nowhere mentioned in the *Ethics* or *Politics*) is the result of mutual ingratitude between the city and the great man.[14] The Graces and natural right are conjoined; together they replace the divine in justice. Aristotle pushes to their limits the solely human grounds and supports for the highest achievements of social and individual self-sufficiency.

Grace is a giving that does not have some return in mind.[15] It would be simply another form of exchange if it were performed for the sake of receiving a reward, even the reward of gratitude. But Aristotle says that the Graces require the initiation of a favor and not merely the repayment of one. Because the hero risks and sometimes gives his life for the city, his action must be gracious in a literal sense. The initiation of a favor by the city, however, would conflict with justice (1131a25–32). With regard to freely given favors, the Graces are a reminder to the citizens, not to the city. Alcibiades' failure to understand this constitutes his one lapse of prudence. The city's gratitude on this account must be of the strongest kind. The elevation of the defender to almost divine status is necessary in order that the defender not devote his talents to merely private challenges. Athens' failure to recognize this in Alcibiades' case was one of its many foolish acts.[16]

Grace as gratitude, moreover, is necessary for the city both to preserve itself and to live well. In addition to heroes, the city needs benefactors, especially those who are munificent. Outfitting the triremes, they help defend the city. Adorning the tragic chorus in purple, they provide the city with beauty in the arts. The munificence of the gift is the donor's original reward, but the city cannot say to the giver, as the tyrant Dionysius said to the musician, "I have already paid you by the pleasure I have given you." The city must honor the donor "or else there is no sharing and it is sharing which makes [the city] last."[17]

Requiting evil with evil is the province of justice and the laws. Aristotle's passage on the Graces is ambiguous about this kind of requital. If outside the reach of the laws, one evil can be that of undeserved good fortune. Aristotle discusses this in Book II of the *Ethics*. Righteous indignation is pain felt at undeserved flourishing by another; envy is pain at any flourishing by another (1108b1–6). These emotions can be a source of division in the city. The shrine of the Graces is a reminder that the good of the city erases the distinction between righteous indignation and envy, a helpful reminder when one is on the threshold of indignation. The Graces show that the flourishing of any citizen is the flourishing of the city; they exhort one to rejoice in another's good fortune as in the good fortune of a friend. The recipient is reminded, too, to be grateful to the city for his good fortune. His gift to the city constitutes such a recognition and shows all citizens their connection with his good fortune. The Graces, then, indicate a pious relation of giving and honoring, but this relation exists between the citizens and the city rather than between the gods and men.

Aristotle relates contemplation to the divine in Book X of the *Ethics*.[18] Yet even here nothing like the Homeric gods is encountered, and there is no discussion of the need for piety. Contemplation is an activity of the intellect, the divine on the human level. It is self-sufficient and above action, as the gods are. One who contemplates is akin to the gods and is therefore most loved by the gods. This relationship to the gods consists not in the observance of religious rites in humble awe, but in seeking to know and to contemplate all things. The human being must not merely look up to but must also ascend to the level of the gods. While contemplation can be an appropriate and even spirited stance toward the gods, it cannot be a common one: very few can participate in this activity and only alone. The two outlets of the divine, contemplation and gratitude, diverge in their expression. Graditude culminates in gracious reciprocity; contemplation, by its movement toward unchanging self-sufficiency, seems to negate the message of the Graces. Aristotle's twofold depiction of the gods, as both inactive and loving, indicates this divergence. But, as with the spiritedness and piety of the heroes, these two activities expressing the divine are animated by the same desire: immortality. That desire has many forms including that of spiritedness. The city must strive for immortality in self-perpetuation. The citizen too adulates life, as long as he thinks that immortality consists of his body's not dying. The immortality of the philosopher, on the other hand, is his participation in the eternal through contemplation. There is no extrinsic reward for this activity or otherworldly punishment for its absence. Nor does contemplation—although it involves prudence—guard him against chance, ward off misfortune, or preserve the body in its earthly identity.

However, this relationship to the divine through contemplation seems to endanger the very gods who the citizens believe are the guarantors of their immortality.[19] The disjunction between the philosopher and the city lies in the constitutive nature of each: the essence of philosophy is knowledge, of the city its laws; the means of philosophy must be continual questioning, of the city command and obedience. What sort of relationship can there be between the requirements of the two with respect to piety? Since the philosopher must be a part of the city as well as outside it (questioning it and encompassing it through his knowledge), the problem resolves itself into a question of the unity of the city. What can hold the city together? The difficulty

exists not only between the philosopher and the city but also
between the citizen and the city in their different requirements
for self-preservation and for freedom.

The Unity of Spiritedness and Piety

A common belief in the gods, a common piety, could be an
admirable source of unity for the city.[20] The alliance of the city
with the gods, the city claims, gives the citizen a double guarantee of immortality: the citizen will live through the continued
existence and renown of the city and, even with the demise of
the city, the gods will assure his journey beyond this world. The
gods are counted upon to provide the spectrum of self-
preservation to the city, from minimal bodily needs through the
luxuries of good fortune to immortality, however understood.
In connecting immortality to self-preservation, however, the
city—again because its reason for being is the preservation of
the body—necessarily views immortality in terms of the body
and material goods. That this view is, in fact, the opinion of
human immortality held by many shows the general harmony
between most human beings and the city. It also causes, para-
doxically, the profound, almost paralyzing fear of death that
holds most men: if the body is primary, its death is the primary
evil. Finally, it gives rise to unfulfillable hopes that cause these
same adherents to be willing to see others die. The political uses
of piety make the divine subservient to political ends—and to
the wrong political ends. The gods in the service of the political
destroy both the divine and the city. The spiritedness stemming
from such piety knows no distinction between friend and enemy,
knowledge and opinion.

Nor does Aristotle claim that it is piety that holds the city
together. Instead, he refers to the elements that he has severed
from the divine. Proportionate requital holds the city together.
Good for good, evil for evil, and grace are necessary to the city.
The citizens are devoted to the city, and the city preserves the
citizens' freedom. Good citizens are enabled by law to exile bad

citizens. The initiator of a favor to the city is honored above his fellow citizens.

But more than reciprocity is needed to establish unity. The need that holds the city together can be satisfied by imports from abroad (1133a27). Mere exchange of goods can be effected among strangers. The insufficiency of reciprocity is confirmed by Aristotle, who says in Books VIII and IX of the *Ethics* that the claim of justice is superseded by the claim of friendship. The core of political justice is shown to be friendship. Concord or like-mindedness among citizens is the friendship necessary to prevent faction, and concord requires more than justice, exchange, or requital. Concord requires not merely that each person want or think the same thing—for example, it is not concord that each citizen should want to get the highest price possible for his products or as much freedom as possible within the security of the state—but that each want the same thing in relation to the same person. Concord is a distributive or constitutive relation. Only the particular declaration, "I want Pittacus to rule"—and even Pittacus must agree—can evoke the similarity of mind that unites the city. "Concord is, then, about the practical things, those connected to great matters, and capable of being shared by both or by all" (1167a29).

The basis for friendship in the city is spiritedness, "for spiritedness is the capacity of the soul whereby we are friends."[21] Aristotle in the *Politics* reinstates the benefits of spiritedness that he had denigrated in connection with heroic courage. Discussing the desired character or nature of the citizens in the regime according to prayer, Aristotle praises the Greeks. Rather than having only a spirited nature (*thymoeidēs*) and thus being unable to rule politically, or only intelligence and thus being continuously dominated, the Greek nature has both these capacities in an appropriate mixture; thus the Greeks are easily educated in virtue by the legislator. Political rule and freedom are the fitting aims of the good city. It is through spiritedness, Aristotle continues, "that rule and freedom are in all cases acquired: for spiritedness is able to rule and it is indomitable."[22]

The spiritedness whereby citizens are friends is not the

reactive fear or anger of the animal described by Aristotle as epitomizing false courage, nor is it the willful opposition to whatever is not one's own. Political spiritedness exists on the high plane of magnanimity. The magnanimous man occupies the peak of the moral virtues. He claims and deserves the highest honors, but he is moved to act only by those deeds that are great and notable. He chooses to own beautiful but unprofitable things as a sign of self-sufficiency. He speaks freely or with irony because he cares more for the truth than for what people think of him. Although they can be angered by the slights and injuries inflicted by their friends, the magnanimous by nature are harsh only to doers of injustice.[23] Political spiritedness is the source of justice as well as of friendship.

The key to the unity of the city, then, is the magnanimous man, who is spirited and intelligent and thus able to rule and to remain free. If the city is the replacement for the Homeric gods who care for the human things, the magnanimous man replaces the Homeric heroes. But the magnanimous man is above the honors of the city, nor does he fear the city's blame. He is his own complete judge. His actions are inspired by their greatness and not by his desire for honor, although they are the actions which the city honors.[24] Above all, the magnanimous man can provide political rule and freedom in a way that harmonizes these competing elements, that unites the various and dissimilar parts of the city, and that brings together to the extent possible the good of the individual and the common good.

Through his great and notable actions, the magnanimous man provides a focal point for the spiritedness of the many that stems from the love of one's own. Rather than degenerating into an invidious selfishness, the spiritedness led by the magnanimous man is harnessed to the defense of the city. The many and the city are essentially connected: the many the body of the city and its military followers, as the military leaders, the judges, and the deliberators—the decent—are its soul. This brings the city closer to the many: when the many claim that they are the city, there is a truth to this claim that is tied to their shared ends.[25] The magnanimous man provides a more proximate support than the gods for the natural piety of the many, through which they are induced to just action and are inclined toward the divine.

Aristotle does not believe one can simply depend on admiration of the magnanimous man to bring the many to justice. But when he writes of the inability of the many to be made law-abiding by persuasion, his alternative is "laws with teeth," and certainly not a Myth of Er. In the *Metaphysics*, Aristotle scorns using gods as "a means of persuading the many and as something useful for the laws and for matters of expediency."[26] He prefers, perhaps for reasons of piety, that punishment of lawbreakers be administered by human hands. He says that "almost the most necessary and most difficult of all offices is the one concerned with the execution of judgment upon persons cast in suits and those posted as defaulters according to the lists, and with the guarding of the prisoners [literally, "of the bodies"]." Human law-enforcers have the most difficult of all offices. They cannot see into human hearts, and a political rather than a divine system of punishment provides a temporary but fortunately unreliable ring of Gyges to the unjust; nevertheless, the judgment of human law-enforcers is here and now, and their lacunae do not call into question the justice, impartiality, or the existence itself of the gods. Thus because the many are ruled by their bodies through their passions, and because the many epitomize the body, which is the cause and end of the city, it seems certain that Aristotle's religious arrangements in the city aim toward the gods' representing not reward or retribution but necessity.[27] With this necessity comes a kind of freedom that is not present in Homeric piety. The element of fear is attenuated by the element of responsibility—to a degree the citizens' fate depends on their own actions—and by the fact that the city is present and comprehensible to them. And the city, dependent on the distinction between the possible and the impossible, is able to discern the importance of reason.

While the many are in awe of the power and success of the magnanimous man, the decent are attracted to him through their love of the noble, and it is through this passion that they can be led to virtue. For they are open to the persuasion of reason or intelligence through its intrinsic beauty. When Aristotle speaks of the education of the decent in Book X of the *Ethics* he is completely silent about piety. What takes its place is an education in the noble or the beautiful. This education is more in keeping with the true nature of the divine and does not have the drawbacks in respect to the decent that conventional piety does. It is an education toward an object that is an end in itself. It requires activity on the part of the educated, who must search out the beautiful and strive to make their own lives noble. The standard is something outside themselves, not self-gratification. Because it leads the educated outside themselves, it keeps them from making the comparisons with others that can lead to righteous indignation.[28]

It must be stressed that acting for the sake of the noble is not the same as acting for the sake of honor. As is the case with courageous actions, the judgment of the nobility of one's actions depends on one's own knowledge of nobility or beauty: it does not depend on the favor of others—and it is thus vulnerable neither to the objections that make honor an unsuitable standard nor to the fluctuating demands of honor that make the life of the seeker of honor uncertain, inconstant, and liable to stray from the guidance of the noble toward the allure of the opinions of others.[29]

Moreover, an education in the noble or the love of the beautiful provides the right education about the gods. Most references to the gods in the *Ethics* either emphasize the remoteness of the gods from human affairs or liken human beings to the gods: imitation is the sincerest form of piety. Aristotle's discussion of education in Book VIII of the *Politics* is also silent about piety. The gods are mentioned only as standards to learn from in the arts; such learning is the political parallel to emulation of the gods by seeking to know and by the activity of contemplation. The gods are the intellect; their reflection is the beautiful. That customary piety is rejected as the proper education for the decent is playfully corroborated by Aristotle when he rejects the Phrygian mode of music as "enthusiastic" and as appealing to those passions that lead to frenzy. Rather than speaking explicitly of the Phrygian mode, Aristotle criticizes the Phrygian composer Olympus. Aristotle is so fond of homonymic jokes that one may suspect he is criticizing Olympus, the home of the Homeric gods, for engendering excessive enthusiasms; he thus warns against an education in Homeric piety.[30]

The highest human attainment on the political level lies in the exercise of intellectual virtue of prudence and moral virtue of magnanimity, or greatness of soul. Prudence and magnanimity are each shared by the magnanimous man and the philosopher. The philosopher has a theoretical prudence with regard to the knowledge of the good political life; he has a practical prudence with regard to his own good. His magnanimity lies in the truth and greatness of his activity and in the relation of that activity to all human beings. The magnanimous man, through the greatness of his soul and his love of the truth, is receptive to philosophy, although his first object is the spirited care for his own city, and his love of truth stems from the concern for his own soul. He can act as a link between the city and philosophy and can bring to the city, as the philosopher cannot, the benefits of philosophy, rendered safe—but thereby less true—for the city. Moreover, the magnanimous man can relay to the decent the noble character of the political likenesses of philosophy's truths. In this indirect way, philosophy provides the true basis for self-preservation: self-love based on one's own goodness. The magnanimous man provides an object for the concord of desires; in so doing, he provides for the true basis for friendship in the city: the most just articulation possible among the parts of the city.[31]

The shrine of the Graces represents the relation of spiritedness and piety to the city. In Greek myth, the Graces were associated with Aphrodite, Eros, and Dionysus. In Athens the armed youths swore their allegiance to their country before the Graces.[32] The many and the decent need each other for the defense of the city. They also need each other to give the city's justice the elements it needs, exchange and virtue—though this is perhaps not so easily remembered. The Graces, connected in Athens both with the requirements of war and with the beauties of nature and the refinements of art, serve to remind of the mutual need on all levels of those who are part of the city. Perhaps the most urgent need is to honor the city's outstanding human beings, the magnanimous. Through their command of the many, they preserve the city from both attack and corruption. Through their leadership of the decent, they give the city just rulers and cause it to live well. Through their openness to philosophy and their moderation of its truths for the sake of their own city, they allow the city to participate in immortality.

Notes

1. Aristotle, *Nicomachean Ethics*, trans. H. Rackman, 2d edition (Cambridge: Harvard University Press, 1933), hereafter cited as *NE*, 1115a5 ff. For some passages I have used my own translation. All parenthetical citations in the text refer to the *Nichomachean Ethics*, unless otherwise attributed.
2. *NE* 1116b23–1117a3. These similes, which to say the least are unexpected, are only the surface glimmers of the strangeness of Aristotle's entire presentation of courage and its extremes.
3. Certainty about Achilles' superiority is expressed by Hector's father and mother before Hector faces Achilles. Although one may doubt the wisdom of the timing of their observations, Hector's parents seem to have a greater awareness of the actual situation than he does.
4. The two types of political courage are on the surface more different from each other than are the separate categories of the experienced and the sanguine. If they had been counted separately, however, spiritedness would not have been the central pseudo-courage, nor would it have corresponded numerically to Hesiod's golden age. Cf. Leo Strauss, *The City and Man* (Chicago: University of Chicago Press, Midway Reprints, 1977), pp. 129–30.
5. The Greek for *birds* also means *omens*, because birds were the primary source of signs given by the gods.
6. Cf. Robert K. Faulkner, "Spontaneity, Justice and Coercion: On *Nicomachean Ethics*, Books III and V," in *Coercion*, Nomos XIV, eds. J. Roland Pennock and John W. Chapman (Chicago: Aldine-Atherton, 1972), pp. 81–106.

7. *NE* 1128b11–13. The desire for honor as a cause of political courage is in fact the same: glory prolongs life.

8. *NE* 1128b10–35. Cf. Thomas L. Pangle, *The Laws of Plato* (New York: Basic Books, 1980), p. 518, n. 55; see also pp. 439–41, 448–49.

9. The third passage is from the *Odyssey*, the context of which may indicate the kind of spiritedness which underlies the love of one's own family or country. The last passage, origin unknown—"his blood boiled"—seems to depict the spiritedness which is indistinguishable from anger. These passages do serve to indicate the great range of meaning of the word *thymos*, from love to hatred, from body and soul. Cf. Richard John Cunliffe, *A Lexicon of the Homeric Dialect* (Norman: University of Oklahoma Press, 1963), s.v. *thymos*.

10. *NE* 1116b3–23; 1144b24–30. Cf. 1107a9–27. Aristotle uses the word *deos* (terror—the sensation of fear) instead of *phobos*. *Phobos* connotes a display of fear, especially through flight. Knowing himself to be without *deos*, the courageous man is free to flee the battle for the sake of wise strategy. Cf. *Liddel and Scott's Greek-English Lexicon*, abridged (Oxford: Clarendon Press, 1871, 1963), s.v. *phobos*.

11. Gauthier and Jolif explain the thrust of *hypokenein* as underscoring the fearful character of that which the courageous man endures: he stands, as it were, underneath the object he faces. Even if he has fallen, he still remains defiant. René Antoine Gauthier and Jean Yves Jolif, eds. and trans., *L'Ethique à Nicomaque*, 2d ed. (Louvain: Publications Universitaires, 1970), vol. II, p. 225.

12. Aristotle, *Politics*, trans. H. Rackham (Cambridge: Harvard University Press, 1967), hereafter cited as *Pol.*; 1328b12–13, 1329a28–34; 1329a35–39; 1322b18–38; 1299b14–1300a10. Leo Strauss, op. cit., pp. 27–28.

13. Aristotle's use of Brasidas as his example indicates the importance of the city to one's pursuit of glory: Thucydides emphasizes that Amphipolis intensified Brasidas' honors by obliterating the honors previously given its founder. The Brasidas example complicates the question of honors, however, because Amphipolis' tribute was also due to its fear of Sparta. This sort of complication is intrinsic to the natural right of the city. Thucydides, V.x–xi. *The Oxford Classical Dictionary*, 2d edition (Oxford: Clarendon Press, 1972), hereafter cited as *OCD*; s.v. "Brasidas."

14. *OCD*, s.v. "Alcibiades." Leo Strauss, "Preliminary Observations on the Gods in Thucydides' Work," in *Studies in Platonic Political*

Philosophy (Chicago: University of Chicago Press, 1983), pp. 102–04. Aristotle's silence on Alcibiades might be a sign that he writes primarily from the point of view of the city in these works.

15. Aristotle, *The "Art" of Rhetoric*, trans. John Henry Freese (Cambridge: Harvard University Press, 1967), hereafter cited as *Rhet.*; 1385a20. Aristotle distinguishes this type of action, benevolence, from the kind of action arising from pity or the feeling that a similar evil might befall oneself. *Rhet.* 1385b18. *Pol.* 1320a25–b16; 1267a38–b9; 1263b5–14.

16. Joseph Cropsey, "Justice and Friendship in the *Nicomachean Ethics*" *Political Philosophy and the Issues of Politics* (Chicago: University of Chicago Press, 1977), pp. 261–62, 264. Alcibiades is mentioned in the *Rhetoric* as having descendants who became mad: his offspring were for him an even less certain road to immortality than his political deeds. *Rhet.* 1390b30.

17. *NE* 1122a34–35; 1122b6; 1122b15–35; 1164a14–23.

18. *NE* 1177a12–1178a2; 1179a23–33.

19. *Aristotle's Metaphysics*, trans. Hippocrates G. Apostle (Bloomington: Indiana University Press, 1966), hereafter cited as *Met.*, 1072b14–30; 1025b1–1026a33. *Pol.* 1266b31–1267a18. *NE* 1111b21–23; 1124a13–17; 1177b27–1178a2.

20. Cf. Jean-Jacques Rousseau, *Social Contract*, I.vi–vii.

21. *Pol.* 1327b41.

22. *Pol.* 1327b18–1328a22. If spiritedness facilitates rule as well as preventing domination, one might wonder what the place of intellect is. But although the ability to rule belongs to spiritedness, the ability to rule politically requires intelligence in addition. Aristotle, I believe, is pointing to the distinction between general domination and the power to arrange and govern a city so that it achieves virtue, that is, the good of the city and of its citizens. Needless to say, this latter would require knowledge of what virtue is. Again, the importance of reason as an aspect of any virtue is made clear.

23. *NE* 1123a33–25a17. *Pol.* 1328a8–18. Cf. pp. 8–9 and n. 10 above.

24. *NE* 1124a1–20; 1124b23–27; 1125a11–13. *Pol.* 1312a22–30. That the philosopher is also magnanimous is shown, among other ways, by the words Aristotle uses to describe both the magnanimous man and Socrates.

25. *Pol.* 1290b21–1291b13.

26. *Met.* 1074b1–10. *NE* 1179b11–21; 1179b30–1180a4; 1180a4–24.

27. *Pol.* 1321b40–1322a34. *NE* 1180a4–15. Cf. Alfarabi, *The Philosophy*

of Plato and Aristotle, trans. M. Mahdi (Ithaca: Cornell University Press, 1965), II.x.

28. *Pol.* 1340a14–19, *NE* 1179b4–11, 30–32. *The noble* and *the beautiful* are the same word in Greek.

29. *NE* 1095b23–30; 1124a5–13.

30. *NE* 1101b10–35, etc. *Pol.* 1339b7–9; 1340a8–12, b5; 1341b2–8; 1342a33–b12. *Met.* 984b15; 1065b3–4; 1074b24–25.

31. *NE* 1140a25–29, 1141a29–34, b25–30; 1123b35–1124a5, 25–29; 1166a15–23. For another view of virtue in the city, cf. Thomas A. Pangle, op. cit., pp. 385, 389, 399. The magnanimous man bridges the city through the creation of a tension within himself—rather than a domination—of the disparate elements of his soul, and a tension within the city of—rather than a tyranny over—the disparate natures of its inhabitants. Cf. *NE* 1124b7–8, 25–27 with *Pol.* 1312a39.

32. *OCD,* s.v. "Charitēs. "Catherine B. Avery, ed., *The New Century Handbook of Greek Mythology and Legend* (New York: Appleton-Century-Crofts, 1972), s.v. "Charitēs."

HARVEY C.
MANSFIELD, JR.

V

Machiavelli and the Modern Executive

The modern executive, whether in politics or business, feels a vague but uneasy kinship with Machiavelli that he rarely seeks to define or escape by reading the works of Machiavelli. Perhaps in his mind he delegates this task to the scholars of Machiavelli, most of whom assume that Machiavelli, despite his reputation as the philosopher of scheming evil, was neither a deep thinker nor a teacher of anything to make us uneasy. Whether out of complacency, pride, or fastidiousness, scholars have not accepted this commission and have not explored the instinctive kinship between Machiavelli and the modern executive. If they had done so, they might have found so precise a kinship as would compel them to consider whether Machiavelli might actually be the author of the modern executive. For not only do the two share an attitude and certain methods but also Machiavelli is the first writer on politics to use the word "execute" frequently and thematically in its modern sense.

What is that modern sense? An answer requires a brief consideration of Machiavelli's fundamental notions; then I connect these to Machiavelli's uses of "execute" and develop his notion of *esecuzioni* and the executive.

Machiavelli was not the first political philosopher to make a theme of execution. Marsilius of Padua in his *Defensor Pacis* presents all government as executive of the will of the sovereign people. Marsilius was heir to the tradition of Aristotle, and although Aristotle made little or nothing of executive power, Marsilius remained true to him by subordinating executive power to natural law or natural right, so that executive power never escapes the supervision of law and morality. But Marsilius's and Aristotle's subordination or belittling of the executive in favor of law does not mean that they were blind to the problematic character of law.

That law cannot attain what it attempts is the problem to which the modern notion of executive power is a solution. Law is too universal to be rational, and it needs assistance from outside to specify what is reasonable in each case, which may be against the spirit as well as the letter of the law. Even if law were rational, it would need help in demonstrating its rationality against human beings' stubborn insistence on having things their own way. When law encounters this stubbornness, it resorts to universality and says: you are treated the same as everyone else. Thus the second difficulty feeds the first, and law introduces a problem it cannot resolve on its own.

Executive power is only one solution to the problem of law. Another solution is Aristotle's kingship, which is still to be found in Marsilius.[1] The kingship of the good man or the best man is above the law because of his virtue. Although impossible or impracticable, this kingship reminds us that law never attains virtue, it aims at virtue. If it could be shown—and Aristotle is doubtful about this—that virtue is man's perfection and that man's perfection makes a necessary contribution to nature as a whole, then the kingship of the good man would be according to nature. One would then have the ground on which to assert that departure from the law in the direction of this kingship is not tyrannical but is in accord with natural right, that the problem of law can be resolved, or at least can be treated, with regard to the virtue that our nature permits us.

Machiavelli does not merely doubt this assertion, he denies it. Of his many and various statements by indirection, he says the most in his resounding silence on natural right or natural law, neither of which does he ever mention in any of his works. This is his most evident difference from Marsilius. Indeed, political science neither of his time nor of his tradition gives precedent or excuse for this silence, which cannot be inadvertent.[2]

With this silence Machiavelli calls forth from the "context" into which he is often squeezed today, such as makes his thought appear derivative and harmless, to say something extraordinary and profoundly unsettling. He agrees with Aristotle that law is not enough but denies that departure from it can be justified by natural right; without a trace of squeamishness, indeed with evident relish, he swallows the conclusion that tyranny is necessary to good government. Since law cannot demonstrate its reasonableness, it needs force; since nature does not supply or justify this force, men must find or generate their own. In repeated, sensational acts of execution, men can compel obedience to the law by exercising force beyond the law. These acts, which Machiavelli calls *esecuzioni*, have so to speak nothing to do with either law or justice. Whereas in Aristotle what is beyond law is above it, in Machiavelli what is beyond law is below it. Aristotle always respects the law and requires that even the kingship of the best man adopt it. Machiavelli openly mocks the law; although he does not deny the need for good laws (See *D* I.33), he asserts that good arms are enough to ensure good laws (*P* 12).

While never referring to natural right, Machiavelli does mention nature and, as everyone knows, speaks frequently of virtue.[3] But his nature and virtue are not those of Aristotle or the tradition of classical political science. For Machiavelli, nature is understood as, or is replaced by, the necessity that forces us to gain nutriment, safety, and glory;[4] virtue becomes the habit or faculty or quality of anticipating that threefold necessity. The transformation of virtue required for its new function, in which it is no longer either an end in itself or devoted to human perfection, is indicated by the reluctance of Machiavelli's translators to render his *virtu* as virtue. They call it ingenuity or valor or vigor, thereby revealing that something new is intended while concealing the fact that Machiavelli calls it *virtue*.

In anticipating necessity, virtue for Machiavelli has a twofold character that is responsible for the peculiar ambivalence of the modern executive. The executive is strong but claims to be acting on behalf of a will or force that is stronger.[5] Virtue overcomes necessity and in this sense is understood in opposition to nature (by contrast to Aristotelian natural right), but to overcome necessity virtue makes use of necessity, and in this sense is understood in obedience to nature[6] (also by contrast to Aristotle's natural right, which permits human choice). Thus, to anticipate necessity, you must get ahead of the other fellow; when you have succeeded in *assicurarsi* ("securing yourself"), you have defeated the other fellow but not the necessity of defeating him—and others after him. Your virtue is both strong and weak: strong because you have chosen to do what you would eventually have been forced to do; weak because you had no other choice. Accordingly, Machiavelli speaks of executors with ambivalence. At one point (*P* 6) he describes Moses as a "mere executor of the things that had been ordained by God" but later (*P* 26) he praises "the virtue of Moses" in taking advantage of an opportunity afforded him; and elsewhere he says that Moses was forced to kill countless men who out of envy were opposed to "his designs" (*D* III. 30), that is, Moses' not God's. To balance the single mention in his writings of "mere executor" in *The Prince*, the need for *uno ostinato esecutore* ("a determined executor") in the *Discourses on Livy* (III. 1).

The Machiavellian executive is more usually known as the Machiavellian prince, and of course more usually called so by Machiavelli. But we shall find that the ways of the prince are essential elements of the modern executive; Machiavelli's frequent use of execute perhaps in response to Marsilius is far from incidental to his main conceptions. But *esecuzione* is fundamental for the modern executive. Seven elements of the modern executive originate in Machiavelli: the political use of punishment, which demands an outsized executive; the primacy of war and foreign affairs over peace and domestic affairs, which greatly increases the occasions for emergency powers; the use of indirect government, when ruling is perceived to be executing on behalf of someone or some group other than the ruler; the erosion of differences among regimes as wholes, through the discovery or development of techniques of governing applicable to all regimes; the need for decisiveness, for government is best done suddenly; the value of secrecy in order to gain surprise; and the necessity of the single executive, "one alone," to take on himself the glory and the blame. Each of these elements can be contrasted to Aristotle's notions to see how Machiavelli's executive is revolutionary, and all elements are illustrated in Machiavelli's use of the term execute.[7]

Political Punishment

Among the many sensational statements with which Machiavelli takes delight in shocking his readers, few are more eyecatching than his pronouncement that "mixed bodies" such as sects, republics, and kingdoms need periodic "executions" to return them toward their beginnings in order to rid them of corruption (*D* III.1). This is the most prominent of his remarks on executive power. The executions in question are both killings and punishments of lawbreakers—executions in both primary meanings of the word which coincide in capital punishments. These executions do punish criminals, but they are praised for their "good effects" and not for their accuracy in retribution. It does not seem important that a formal law has been broken, still less that procedural regularity has been preserved. If a law has not been transgressed, then "orders" or institutions need to be revived when they have been used corruptly merely for self-advancement; indeed, it is human ambition and insolence that need to be restrained, rather than actual violations of the law punished. Machiavelli even promises that had Rome been able to schedule important executions every ten years, "it would follow of necessity that she would never have become corrupt" (*D* III.1, see III.22). He does not entertain any doubts from the scrupulous as to whether deserving criminals would always keep to his schedule. What matters is that the executions be "excessive and notable." Soon after Machiavelli drops the reference to laws and orders as explicitly as only he can: "after a change of state, either from republic to tyranny or from tyranny to republic, a memorable execution against the enemies of the present conditions is necessary" (*D* III.3). The execution may as well be tyrannical as legal, provided that it be memorable. The good effects of such executions are to revive "that terror and that fear" (*D* III. 1) that has faded from vivid memory since beginnings of the sect, republic, or kingdom.

Thus criminal justice is used—why not say perverted?—for political effect. The effect is not marginal: we would lose something significant by foregoing executions for the sake of legality; memorable executions are crucial to the salvation of the regime. Aristotle disposes his thought entirely to the contrary. In the *Ethics* he distinguishes criminal justice from distributive justice, and he connects distributive justice to politics and political justice. Criminal justice, hardly discussed, is categorized with the justice of contracts as a kind of transaction (*NE* 1131a2) and is left aside as neutral or consequential to the politics of a city. In the *Politics* little is said of punishment and nothing is made of the offices of punishment because Aristotle wants to remove politics from subservience to punitive gods. For Aristotle, the true beneficiaries of an enlarged executive power would be the priests; he wanted to keep them subordinate to the offices of the regime in which human choice and deliberation could prevail.[8] The sacral cities around him were not to be encouraged in their desire for revenge and punishment. Aristotle's anticlericalism has to be discerned through the delicate conciseness of his rhetoric and through the moderation necessitated by his opposition to philosophers. In the different circumstances that Marsilius faced, with the papacy a "singular cause" of disunion, Aristotle's subdued dislike came out into the open.

Machiavelli easily surpassed both Aristotle and Marsilius in anticlericalism, and he wished to hold priests under political control, but he thought it necessary to express or purge revenge and then restrain it through fear rather than justice. The fear generated by the return toward the beginnings substitutes for fear of God, which Machiavelli remarks is used by priests but not felt by them: "they do the worst they can, because they do not fear the punishment they do not see and do not believe in" (*D* III. 1). Memorable executions not only restrain the ambition and insolence of those active in politics but also purge the people of the ill humors they feel against a prominent citizen. The accusations Machiavelli says are necessary to keeping republics in freedom definitively conclude with an "execution" that must be made without the "private" or "foreign" forces that priests, especially, have at their call (*D* I.7). Similarly, in *The Prince*, Machiavelli explains that the Florentine people, through too much mercy, once allowed disorders to spread that could have been quelled with a very few examples of cruelty. Disorders, Machiavelli points out, harm a whole people, but "the executions that come from a prince hurt one particular individual (*P 17*). Machiavelli's lesson is that too much love leads to cruelty, but the economy of single executions should no more be mistaken for justice than their memorableness. In fact, when it comes to punishing a multitude, Machiavelli does not hang back. He praises the greatness of the Roman republic and "the power of its executions" among which the decimation of a multitude was "terrible" (*D* III.49). For when a whole multitude deserves punishment, and only a part receives it because there are too many to punish, one does wrong to those punished and inspires the unpunished to err on another occasion. But when a tenth selected by chance are killed, and all deserve it, the punished lament their bad luck and the unpunished are afraid to misbehave the next time.

This discussion could easily be interpreted (or misinterpreted if one wishes to preserve Machiavelli's innocence) as a political appropriation of the Christian doctrine of original sin, just as the memorable execution could be seen as a suggested use for the Christian doctrine of redemption. Machiavelli, it would appear, is not above reviving states through a notion of punishment taken from the very institution that he accuses of having "rendered the world weak and given it in prey to wicked men" (*D* II.2: see I pr.). The modern doctrine of executive power begins in Machiavelli's appropriation, for worldly advantage and human use, of the power that men had been said to exercise in executing God's will. At the end of Machiavelli's dialogue *The Art of War*, the principal interlocutor Fabrizio laments that nature either should not have given him the knowledge of how to revive and expand states or should have given him the faculty of "executing" it (*AW* VII.367b). Since nature gives men knowledge without the faculty of execution, men must execute on their own, using (in Machiavelli's famous phrase) their own arms; they must not wait for help from God and nature. But they have at their disposal knowledge from nature, the knowledge of their own nature, including truths discerned and misapplied by Christian doctrine, now to be interpreted "according to virtue" (*D* II.2) by Machiavelli. Machiavelli attempted to make "the world," that is, mankind, strong again, but he did so by showing it how to submit to its own nature.

Because God or nature cannot be relied on to help execute men's laws, there being no natural law or natural right behind those laws, the power of execution must expand. Execution must lose the close subordination to law that it retains in Aristotle and Marsilius. Only once in Machiavelli's major writings, I believe, does "execute" occur with "law" in such a way that it is clear a law is being executed (*FH* VII.3). In other cases, the following are said to be executed: authority (*FH* I.16), undertaking (*FH* VI.29, VIII.4) office (*FH* V.21), thought (*FH* VII.34), conspiracy (*FH* VIII.4, 5, *D* III.6—of which more later), desire (*FH* VIII.26), public decisions (*FH* VIII. 29, *D* I.33), important thing (*D* I.49), everything (*D* II.2), these things (*AW* V.331b), preparations (*AW* I.274b), practice (*AW* I.303b), policy (*AW* VII.362b), evil (*P* 19), command (*AW* VI.348a), and commission (*FH* IV.10, *D* III.6). Only the last two can be called weak uses of execute.[9] In many more cases, what is executed is left unstated—clearly a strong use (see *D* III.27, *FH* II.12, 25, 26, 34, III.14, 19, VII.6, 21, 32, 34, VIII. 36). Nor must we forget the notable executions already discussed, from which law is conspicuously absent (*D* III.1, 3, see also *FH* II.34, III.19, 21, IV.30). In sum, these uses of execute[10] add up to an outsized executive who, because the function of punishment must be understood politically, is not confined to carrying out the law. Executions do indeed cause laws to be obeyed; in a general sense they are subordinate to law. But *legal* executions do not suffice, and law must accept the help of illegality to secure its enforcement.

The Primacy of War and Foreign Affairs

Once execution is liberated from its clear subordination to law and its connection to justice, it becomes available as a remedy for emergencies generally, not merely for the exigencies of law enforcement. Such emergencies can arise from sudden foreign dangers as easily as from obstreperous ambition at home, and to be met they require a large delegation of power. One of Aristotle's five kinds of kingship is the general, with powers delegated for war; he is a regular official who ruled in accordance with law.[11] By contrast, Machiavelli praises the Roman practice of creating a dictator in emergencies, "when an inconvenience has grown in a state or against a state" (D I.33). This gives "power to one man who could decide without any consultation and could execute his decisions without any appeal."[12] Machiavelli denies that dictatorial authority is harmful or that it brought tyranny to Rome, as had been alleged. The dictator was very useful not only when the Roman republic was threatened from without but also—now Machiavelli reverses the moral ground— "in the increase of its empire."[13]

Thus, just as with regard to punishment Machiavelli steps past the difficulties of law enforcement to embrace the necessity of injustice, so with foreign affairs he turns from dealing with emergencies that may arise from any state minding its own business to those that a state with imperial ambition necessarily seeks out or creates to serve as pretexts (see D III.16). Whereas Plato's *Republic* and Aristotle's *Politics* deal summarily with foreign affairs, Machiavelli's *Discourses on Livy* according to its announced plan is half devoted to foreign affairs and at least as much of *The Prince*. In the Middle Ages, the classical tradition had to be modified by Arabs and Jews to take account of their relations with gentiles. It had to be adapted by Christians to the broad sway of emperors and popes. These modifications introduced new matter for foreign policy, yet did not affect the status of justice, hence the primacy of domestic affairs. But when fear replaces justice as the ground for politics, as in Machiavelli, acquisition is loosed from restraint, and political science assumes the task of explaining to princes how they must acquire and keep their states and to republics how they must overcome corruption and expand. Governments must be taught to treat their own peoples as they would treat foreign peoples subject to them—not necessarily badly but not with trust and justice. The notable executions that perpetuate states, together with the dictator's power to execute his own decisions, which expands states, indicate Machiavelli's new emphasis on survival in politics. Classical political science, assuming that all regimes moved through a cycle and were fated to die, judged regimes by how they behaved, not by how long they survived. Machiavelli dismisses the cycle because states would surely become subject to better-ordered neighbors instead of suffering through their own ills in isolation (DI.2).[14] His new domestic policy justifies the primacy of foreign policy, and both are supported by expanded executive power.

Execution as Universal Technique

The best regime, which is the theme of classical political science, does not exist according to Machiavelli. The natural right that would be required to elaborate the best regime, even if it could be done only in speech, does not exist according to him. He disdains such "imaginary republics and principalities" (P 15) and asserts that in all human affairs one inconvenience can never be cancelled without giving rise to another (D I.6). His concern is with actual regimes and their deeds, not with the speeches in which they claim to be best, to be wholes, and to advance the common good. These claims give regimes their distinctive characters; they were seized on by classical political science as means of understanding capable of being refined to measures of judgment.[15]

Machiavelli, who rarely speaks of regimes (there are two instances in FH II.11, 32), abandons the classical classification of six regimes (see D I.2) and adopts from Roman tradition the distinction between republics and principalities (*P* 1). But in making use of this distinction, he does not preserve the characteristic opposition between republics and principalities in what they claim against each other. He makes light both of the typical republican hatred for the "name of the prince" and the "name of king" and of princely disdain for the fickleness of popular government (*D* I.58, II.2). He also erodes the traditional distinction in such phrases as "princes in the republic" and "civil principality" which imply that republics are in need of princes and that principalities can be considered as republics. Republics and principalities converge in this way because both are to be judged not by their contrasting claims of virtue and justice, but by a single standard, the "effectual truth" of those claims, their ability to acquire glory and maintain security. By this standard the boastful claims of regimes are reduced to their effect in producing benefits rather than taken seriously and even amplified as possible elements of the best regime. And the benefits of republics and principalities do not include the honor of living in a republic as opposed to under a prince, or the reverse; the form of government is not an end of government.

Accordingly, though Machiavelli speaks of virtue or goodness in republics, he does not speak of republican virtue, in which devotion to republicanism as a form or regime is identifiable apart from the benefits of republics. He does express a preference for republics over principalities, but it is carefully qualified: the common good "is not preserved if not in republics" (*D* II.2). But the common good of a republic does not extend to its neighbors, since to be conquered by a republic is the hardest slavery, and it is not really common, since it consists of oppression of the few by the many. Thus, when Machiavelli says that in republics everything "is executed to its purpose," whereas what helps a prince most often harms the city (*D* II.2), this must be balanced against his statement praising the "more merciful" prince Cesare Borgia because he knew how to confine his executions to a "very few examples" by contrast to the well-meaning republican Florentines, whose leniency harmed the whole people of Pistoia (*P* 17). More important than regimes are the two diverse humors or natures of princes and peoples to be found in both republics and principalities: the princes' desire to command, and the peoples' desire not to be commanded (*P* letter dedicatory, 9; *P* I.5). The success of government in either form requires prudent management of these two humors.

Or should one say that the advantage is to republics because, as Machiavelli asserts, "a republic has greater life and good fortune for a longer time than a principality" (*D* III.9)? Again, nothing is said about the greater lawfulness of a republic, nor indeed (by contrast to *D* II.2) about the common good. And why do republics live longer? Republics can be accommodated to diverse situations better than a principality because they have at their disposal a diversity of citizens instead of just one prince. But their institutions (or orders) would not permit them to make use of this diversity, given their notorious slowness to decide (*D* I.34, 59), if their institutions did not include the office of dictator, or something like it, which enables them to give responsibility to one person with the qualities needed at the moment. The dictator both is and is not an order. Machiavelli says that the executions of an accusation (which require a dictator or someone similar) are useful because they occur "ordinarily" without resort to private or foreign forces (*D*I.7). He then praises the Roman republic for instituting dictators for immediate executions in an "important thing," when the ordinary course would cause delay (*D* I.49) or when one man is needed to decide by himself without appeal (*D* I.33). Between these passages Machiavelli has shown that the orders of a republic become corrupt, and its authority goes stale, if ordinary means are not revived with "extraordinary means." So far from ruining republics (*D* I.7, 34), extraordinary means are necessary to them (*D* I.18, II.16). Such means culminate in the "notable and excessive" (*D* III.1) and "memorable" executions (*D* III.3) we have discussed, which require taking up an "extraordinary authority" (*D* III.3), "without depending in any law that stimulates you to any execution" (*D* III.1). The ordinary course of orders depends on occasional or periodic resort to the extraordinary for the renewal that gives a republic long life, indeed promises it perpetuity (*D*

III.22). Thus the distinction between lawful and unlawful is transformed into a continuum from ordinary to extraordinary, which allows or requires republics to exchange their lawfulness for long life. To do this, republics must incorporate the principality; the Roman republic was a succession of "countless most virtuous princes" (*D* I.20). Its long life, in Machiavelli's interpretation, was due to its having combined with the princely state to secure the advantages of quick execution. But one could as easily say that a principality could combine with a republic in order to have, when necessary, a quick change of prince. Because of the need for executions, the inner workings of politics are not determined by its outward face.

Indirectness

When government claims to be merely executive, like Moses, who was said to be a "mere executor of the things ordained by God" (*P* 6), its inner workings pretend to take direction from an outside authority. But as execution proves to require a "determined executor" (*D* III.1), the inner workings move on their own, producing memorable executions when necessary as surprises for the sake of greater effect. Machiavelli's executive government is not ordinarily visible, whereas in the Aristotelian regime the form or the look of politics shows the character of politics, so that political reality in general corresponds to political appearance. But Machiavelli's government is not simply invisible, because government cannot work without making an impression and thus cannot always hide itself behind authority. The inner workings of government must be revealed, on extraordinary occasions where government can be impressive because unexpected, in executions that recall to men both why they need government and what government can do to them if they disobey. Only on these occasions does political reality correspond to appearance. But precisely on these occasions, when primal fear is shown to be the first mover of politics—as well as in its ordinary course—government appears as necessity personified, returning men toward their own beginnings to a reawakening. Even at its strongest and most impressive, government acts for men in an executive role. Men do not govern according to principles they choose and profess, as in the classical regime, but they are governed by a prince or princes who remind them, periodically, that necessity is more powerful than principles, hence good effects are more useful than respect for forms. The indirectness of government lies in the fact that necessity must be brought home to each of us (see *AW* VI.348a), ordinarily complacent with partisan notions of how things should be run. Government is neither a choice by the rulers nor an imposition on the ruled but a revelation to each—and not from on high—of what is most powerful, not best, in him. To produce good effects, in the double sense of effects that make an effect, government must have the ambivalence to move on its own ultimately on behalf of the people.

The popular humor is not the desire to rule but the desire not to be ruled; nonetheless, the people must be ruled. This difficulty sets the problem of government: to rule the people without their developing the intolerable sensation that they are being ruled. To accomplish this—for Machiavelli does not doubt he has a "remedy"—he adopts as his fundamental strategy a comical maxim of human perception: "Wounds and every other ill that man causes to himself spontaneously and through choice, hurt much less than those which are done to you by someone else" (*D* I.34). Government should contrive, then, to let its exactions and especially its punishments seem to come from the people being mulcted and punished, at their behest or with their consent. Thus, although the people as such never rule and democracy strictly speaking is impossible, all government, whether republican or princely, must appeal to the people in the manner of the Roman method of accusation that makes the people responsible for the attribution of guilt and execution (*D* I.7). Not only republics but also principalities are counseled by Machiavelli to adopt a generally democratic policy and to rely on the people rather than—or as opposed to—the few (*D* I.49, 55, 58, *P* 20). The contrast to Aristotle's generally aristocratic policy and his appeal to the kingship of the best man is impressive.

An appeal to the people, however, is not an appeal to their good nature or impartiality. It is the means of involving them in the necessities of government they would much rather ignore. Machiavelli praises the Swiss army's method of punishing soldiers "popularly by the other soldiers" (*AW* VI. 345a), for if you want to prevent someone from defending or sympathizing with a criminal, get him to do the punishing. A person will look on punishment differently if he is the executor of it. Another example of executions in an army makes it clear that law and justice are not relevant to them. Rebels from the Carthaginian army were incited by their leaders to kill emissaries from that army together with prisoners they held. This execution was intended to make them "cruel and determined" against the Carthaginians (*D* III.32). Thus, common involvement in a "crime" works as well as common involvement in the punishment of a crime. Both are wounds that the army inflicts on itself, which hurt much less than if executions were carried out by or in the name of, a prince. Machiavelli generalizes (as in *D* III.49) from the decimations by which Roman armies were punished to the proper way to punish a multitude: to make those who are guilty but unpunished watch themselves in the future. Though unpunished, indeed through relief at being unpunished, they nearly punish themselves.

It is a mistake to give the power of executing punishment to a foreigner in hope of finding an impartial judge (*D* I.7, 49, *FH* II.25). The foreigner will simply use executions to gain power for himself. Nor should one give it to the few, for "the few have always been the ministers of the few" (*D* I.49). Rather, executions should be used against the few to hold down their insolence and to dispel envy (*D* III.1, 30, *FH* II.22). The few may be deterred, and the many will be impressed. Executions are never the unprompted act of the people, who would prefer to forget such necessities; to act, the people must be led or given a "head" (*D* I.57). But the people have a love of the sensational that causes them to be easily impressed by bold actions (*D* I.53), and the commission of great crimes is no bar to their favor (*P* 8, 9). In every regime, the people are natural allies of the strong executive who rules them in their name, indirectly.[16]

Suddenness

To make an impression, execution must be sudden. In praising Giovanni and Lorenzo de' Medici, Machiavelli remarked that they were quick to execute (*FH* VII.6, VIII.36). We praise executives as decisive and energetic in their initiatives, bearing witness to the effect of suddenness as it seizes our attention by bringing regular (or ordinary) procedure to an abrupt halt. One of Machiavelli's favorite phrases describes this event: *ad uno tratto* ("at a stroke"). At a stroke the forceful executive can change a situation. People learn that they cannot rely on the familiar (the terrible Roman execution of decimation was decided by lot [*D* III.49]); they must therefore look to the prince. By an impressive stroke the prince thus renews his authority and makes himself a new prince. His personal power, instead of disappearing into the regularity of his laws and ordinary methods, becomes visible; his actions, if sufficiently ambitious, can achieve "the greatness in themselves" that silences criticism (*FH* I pr.). In dealing with hostile parties in Pistoia, the weak Florentines did not know how to follow the first and safest method of simply killing the leaders: "such executions have greatness and generosity" (*D* III.27).

In a paraphrase of Livy that Machiavelli notes should be chewed on by every prince and every republic, he says that in ambiguity and uncertainty over what others want to do, one cannot find words; but once one's mind is made up and one has decided what is to be "executed," it is easy to find the words for it (*D* II.15). One must accommodate words to deeds, not deeds to words; and one does this by acting first, so as to confront others with a new situation. Machiavelli writes of the Roman dictatorship that in time of necessity offered the advantage of immediate executions (*D* I.49). But here Machiavelli goes beyond responding to necessity, advising that one create necessity for others. He says that slow deliberations are always harmful (*D* II.15). This is especially true in conspiracies, where menaces are more dangerous than executions (*D* III.6, p. 200b). Dangers in executing conspiracies arise in part from those who lose heart (*FH* VII.34), but they can be avoided by stepping up the pace of the execution so that the faint-hearted have no time to suffer an attack of conscience (*FH* II.32, *D* III.6, p. 208a). Machiavelli gives two examples of conspiracies that were executed first on fellow conspirators before they were executed on the objects of the conspiracy. The conspirators were told they must join against a tyrant or be reported to him for treason (*D* III.6, p. 204a). In such cases, and in general, the executor makes use of "the necessity that does not allow time" (*D* III.6, p. 206a), that is, time to repent.

In no respect does Machiavelli's executive differ more obviously from Aristotle's regime than in his suddenness. For Aristotle, the central part of the regime was the deliberative, and while deliberate is not the same as slow, deliberate in the sense of slow is the beginning of deliberate in the sense of prudent. The deliberative part, therefore, was chosen and authorized to act through a variety of formalities whose general purpose was to slow the haste of human willfulness by compelling propriety and due process.[17] Machiavelli, to the contrary, advances deliberation into decision (in the usage of his time *diliberazione* meant both deliberation and decision), so that a good deliberation becomes one that issues in a decision, and a good decision is decisive (*D* II.15). Decisive is known and explained after the fact, and while sudden is not the same as prudent, it is a necessary addition to prudence, as that appearance of willfulness that gets prudence obeyed. Machiavelli's executive cuts through the formalities that Aristotle was so careful to emphasize. In so doing, he makes it possible for republics, such as the Roman republic according to his interpretation, not to suffer from the slow motion of excess procedure.

Secrecy

When a committee of the U.S. Congress meets in executive session, it meets in secret. We have seen the connection between execution and secrecy in Machiavelli's discussion of the Roman office of dictator, who executes not only without appeal but also without consultation (*D* I.33). If execution requires surprise, secrecy is clearly necessary. The surprise is not a happy revelation, of course, but something more sinister. Just how sinister execution is may be gauged from the fact that the greatest density of *execute* in the *Discourses on Livy* occurs in the long chapter on conspiracies, III.6 (forty occurrences out of sixty in the entire work; forty-nine together with the related chapters, III.1 and III.3). Whereas Machiavelli speaks only once in his major works of executing a law (*FH* VII.3), he speaks several times of executing a conspiracy (*D* III.6, pp. 201b, 210a, *FH* VIII.5; *Life of Castruccio Castracani*, p. 757b); he orders his entire discussion of conspiracies in that chapter around execution—before, during, and after the deed. As we have seen, the way to keep the secret of a conspiracy is to hasten its execution (*D* III.6, pp. 204a–b; *FH* II.32). The execution of a conspiracy perfectly combines the two meanings of execute, "kill" and "carry out," since the conspiracy is executed when its object is executed. It is almost needless to add that conspiratorial execution takes place in utter illegality.

What is Machiavelli's reasoning for removing execution from its subordination of law, where it had been firmly confined by Marsilius, and enlisting it in the management of conspiracies? Conspiracy itself must be much closer to the essence of government than had been thought hitherto. Machiavelli implies this when he writes that conspiracies are made not only against the prince but also against the fatherland (*patria*) by the prince (*D* III.6). But even this, like so many of his statements, is a mere introduction to his reasoning. Government, according to Machiavelli, is the agent of necessity rather than the minister of justice, because we cannot afford justice. But we like to think that we can afford justice, especially for ourselves, and we often see no need for actions which anticipate that we will not be able to afford justice—actions that anticipate necessity. This is the popular humor that does not desire to rule or command or oppress but desires not to be ruled. The desire not to be ruled constitutes a reluctance to face facts or necessity. Government has the ambivalent task of bringing necessity home to the people, so that they survive, while concealing it from them, so that they are happy and innocent. Machiavelli's remedy is to make government seem to come from the people and its wounds seem self-inflicted. This requires fraud (*P* 18, *D* II.13, III.2, 40) and conspiracy (*P* 19, *D* III.6), not merely as dangerous devices locked away in a cabinet for use by trusted hands only in the worst emergencies but as instruments available generally if not routinely, and to be used without hesitation or scruple.

Conspiracies are comprised, Machiavelli says, of either one or more. But, he continues, if it is one person, it cannot be said to be a conspiracy; rather it is a "firm disposition arising in one man to kill the prince" (*D* III.6, p. 201a). So conspiracies, properly speaking, involve more than one person sharing a secret or knowledge together (*coscienza*). The relationship among conspirators is never that among friends, because men usually deceive themselves in the love they judge that another bears for them; you can never be sure of it unless you test it, and this is most dangerous (*D* III.6, p. 203a). Consequently, at least ordinarily the relationship among conspirators must be that of principal and executives instead of equal friends. The executive or secretary (the connection between secret and secretary should not be forgotten) may be more capable than the principal, so that it becomes unclear who is using whom (*P* 22), but the inequality of the relationship remains. To the extent that for Machiavelli conspiracy underlies all politics, we have again reached a fundamental difference from Aristotle, for whom friendship underlies justice and all politics (*NE* 1155a23–33). Aristotle said that friends do not need justice among themselves, as they are above it; Machiavelli thought that, given the secrets they keep from each other and from themselves, they could not even attain justice.

Uno solo

Machiavelli praised the Roman dictatorship that gave one man the power to execute his own decisions in order to respond quickly to "extraordinary accidents" (*D* I.33, 49). But Machiavelli also praised (in *D* I.9) the original ordering of the Roman republic, attributed by him to Romulus, because it had been accomplished in consequence of Romulus' fratricide by "one alone" (*uno solo*). Both the original ordering and the departures from order necessary to maintain order—by the dictator and by the memorable executions (*D* III.1, 3)—must be done by one person. Why must this be?

Machiavelli says that many are not adept at ordering a thing "since they do not know what is good for it, which is caused by the different opinions among them" (*D*I.9). Thus, it appears that everything must depend on the mind of one man, not because he necessarily knows better than the many, but because it is better to have one opinion than many. The prudent orderer must, like Romulus, contrive to get all authority for himself even if he has to dispose of a wiser brother, since Machiavelli says nothing to indicate that Romulus knew more than Remus. It is better to have one opinion and one authority because, with responsibility focused on one, ambition can be used to promote the common good. If the one succeeds, he will have made a lasting state and deserve glory; if he fails, he can be blamed and accused (*D* I.9), thus purging the hatred of the multitude and, if he is sufficiently important, serving as a memorable execution. Although Machiavelli in his popular humor allows himself to inveigh against ambition (*D* I.37, II pr.), his politics make use of ambition untempered, unabashed, and restrained only by the amition of others. Glory, like fear, individuates men, but also enables them to be enlisted for the common good more readily and surely than through the social virtue of justice: "Those who fight for their own glory are good and faithful soldiers" (*D* I.43, see III.30, 35, 40).

If ambition is to be loosed from moral restraint, however, can it be altogether separated from wisdom? It goes without saying that ambitious princes must be prudent, but then prudence from Machiavelli has ceased to be a moral virtue distinct from cleverness (*P* 15, cf. *NE* 1144a24). Must there not be some prudence beyond the ordinary that justifies Machiavelli's corruption of it in the service of ambition—his own *grandi prudenze*

(*D* II.26)? If government culminates in conspiracy, and conspirators cannot be equal, must there not be a brain behind the
operation, a "rare brain" (*D* I.55), one that does not suffer from
"confusion of the brain" (*D* III.6, p. 207a)? Machiavelli was
aware of the problem that the one who knows politics cannot
execute his knowledge by himself (*AW* VII, p. 367b); he can be
uno solo only in his knowledge. In fact, Machiavelli was preoc-
cupied with the problem of the relationship between the teacher
of politics and the politician. When he says in *The Prince* that
Moses was a mere executor of the things ordained by God (*P*
6), he describes God not as all-powerful but as the "great pre-
ceptor." He devotes a chapter in the *Discourses on Livy* to the
dangers of being alone against many in advising something (*D*
III.35, cf. *P* 6, 22); and the thirty-ninth example in the chapter
on conspiracies (*D* III.6, p. 208a) concerns an unsuccessful attempt by two disciples of Plato to kill two tyrants. In the *Florentine Histories* he describes a poet, inspired by Petrarch, who
sought to be the "executor" of a glorious enterprise to free Rome
from the popes (*FH* VI.29).

     In his own glorious enterprise to bring "common benefit
to each" (*D* I pr.) with the reform of morality and politics,
Machiavelli cannot do everything himself. He cannot be both
teacher and prince. But he can put his knowledge into execution,
not least with his doctrine of execution, so that princes who
follow him become in the deepest sense his executives. This
deepest sense of execution is perfectly compatible with the need
of each prince to be uno solo, because Machiavelli has left space
for princes to win their own glory. They can be determined
executors instead of mere executors, and it is not necessary that
they realize they are executing his knowledge; indeed, it is better
that they do not. As Machiavelli shows, a conspiracy can be
executed even when only one person fully knows its object (*D*
III.6, 204a–b). But to be this person, the only true uno solo, the
distinction must be erased between kingship and tyranny.

     With our hindsight from liberal constitutionalism, Ma-
chiavelli seems to have gone too far. His statements ring true
but his conclusions seem exaggerated, and we fail to take him

seriously. We would like to believe that his insights can be retained and his extremism discarded, that his notion of esecuzione can be absorbed into the modern liberal consitution without the tyrannical requirement of uno solo that may give us a shiver or may merely seem quaint. Machiavelli may have founded the modern doctrine of executive power, but in his extremism he stopped short of developing doctrines of power and of separation of powers. The doctrine of power, in Hobbes' conception, was to make virtuous princes unnecessary by giving any sovereign, virtuous or not, all the power he could want; the separation of powers was developed by Locke and Montesquieu to check the prince by law and by formal institutions. Both doctrines, while accepting much of Machiavellian morality, were directed against the extreme political conclusion demanding space for uno solo. But it is not clear that the development of a doctrine improves it. With the same hindsight from constitutionalism, Machiavelli might have chosen to stand pat. He could have noted that we have found no substitute for virtuous princes (in his sense) and that we obscure this fact with talk of executive power. After our experience of tyranny, however, he might have shivered himself.

Notes

1. Aristotle, *Politics* III, 1284a3–17; Marsilius of Padua, *Defensor Pacis* I.11, 6–7; 14.5, 8–9; II.12, 7–9. See Antonio Toscano, *Marsilio da Padova e Niccolo Machiavelli* (Ravenna: Longo, 1981), pp. 112–113.
2. See *P* 15; *DI.2.* Machiavelli's works will be cited as *P* for *The Prince; D* for *Discourses on Livy; FH* for *Florentine Histories; AW* for *The Art of War. NE* is used in reference to Aristotle's *Nicomachean Ethics.* Page references are to Niccolò Machiavelli, *Tutte le Opere* (Florence: G. Barbera, 1929). See also Leo Strauss, *Thoughts on Machiavelli* (Glencoe, Ill.: Free Press, 1958), pp. 13, 30, 59, 222, 236, 290; Claude Lefort, *Le Travail de l'oeuvre Machiavel* (Paris: Gallimard, 1972), p. 301; Gennaro Sasso, *Studi su Machiavelli* (Naples: Morano, 1967), pp. 50–65.
3. Machiavelli speaks of "natural virtues" in *D* I.56; these might perhaps belong to intelligence in the air which might come to the

defense of mankind by issuing warnings and signs. See Harvey C.
Mansfield, Jr., *Machiavelli's New Modes and Orders; A Study of the
Discourses on Livy* (Ithaca, N.Y.: Cornell University Press, 1979),
ad loc.

4. Cf. Harold D. Laswell's "safety, income and deference," in *Politics,
Who Gets What, When, How* (New York: Meridian, 1958), pp.
13 ff.

5. See Harvey C. Mansfield, Jr., "The Ambivalance of Executive
Power," in J. Bessette and J. Tulis, eds., *The Presidency in the Constitutional Order* (Baton Rouge: Louisiana State University Press,
1981), pp. 314–33.

6. See *D* II.3; III.1.

7. So I call it, not to say that Machiavelli ever made scientific or
academic use of terms that do not equivocate, but rather to suggest
that his favorite phrases deserve study.

8. Aristotle wanted to keep the priests fifth, not first; *Politics* 1322b20–
21; 1328b11.

9. But precisely on "commissions," see Machiavelli's praise for the
Roman Senate's grant of "very great authority" to Fabius in the
Ciminian forest affair; *D* II.33.

10. Machiavelli also uses *sequire* (e.g., *FH* II.20) and *mandare ad effetto*
(*FH* I.24, II.10, VII.23, VIII.5, 23) in the sense of *execute*.

11. *Politics* 1285a4, 1286a3.

12. Cf. Aristotle, *Politics* 1285b1–4.

13. Contrast the beginning to the end of the first paragraph of *D* I.33.

14. Harvey C. Mansfield, Jr., "Machiavelli's Political Science," *The
American Political Science Review*, 75 (1981), 301–02.

15. Aristotle, *Politics* 1280a8–23, 1283a23–b35; Plato, *Laws* 690a–c.

16. Thus for Machiavelli to conceive the dictator as commissioned was
not in contradiction to the prince as sovereign, as Carl Schmitt says;
sovereign by commission is the essence of executive ambivalence.
Schmitt cites *D* I.33 but not *D* III.1. Schmitt, *Die Diktatur* (Berlin:
Duncker und Humblot, 1964), pp. 6–9.

17. Cf. Plato, *Apology* 37a–b.

TIMOTHY
FULLER

VI

Elements of Spiritedness in Hobbes: Honor, Fear, and the Rule of Law

To enter the world of modern political thinking, as one does unequivocally with Hobbes, is to encounter a complex understanding of spiritedness. Self-regulation becomes the hallmark of self-determination, and the restraint of passion becomes the hallmark of virtue. The highest manifestation of self-control is the association of individuals under the rule of law. Although not heroic and decidedly antimartial, this association is the apotheosis of the human spirit become self-conscious and, for Hobbes, confident but sober in its aspirations. Association through the rule of law demonstrates that mankind has been set free from divine tutelage and supposes that freedom and reason are mediated by human will. Spiritedness becomes continual willing to mediate and thus to preserve the conditions in which men honor the providential intention. From this perspective, law-abidingness is a high moral achievement dependent on the individuals' continually willing to regulate their passions as natural beings in favor of civil association: this is spiritedness as willing self-limitation.

In the severe forms of dissatisfaction with this virtuous self-restraint, such as Nietzsche's or Marx's, the rule of law is reinterpreted either as the negotiated settlement of concessions from the strong upon the weak or as the result of the weak combining against their superiors, or as both simultaneously. Here spiritedness is thought to be necessary to a radical social transformation in which the indecisive middle world, the political world, will vanish. Spirit now, but tranquility later. This will be achieved only through abandonment of the formalities and the civilities of the rule-of-law polity. The powerful influence of these radicalisms has led to the distorted view that spiritedness can be found only in revolt, that law-abidingness is nothing but acquiescence in the dailiness of life, a preference for the routine and the inauthentic.

None of these forms of disaffection respects the formal separation of virtue from the pursuit of a stipulated good. One wonders whether these alternatives are recipes for anarchy, feeding each other's hostility to the rule of law that persists as a bar to their final, unmediated struggle to triumph. There is in this a resemblance to Hobbes's understanding that he was surrounded by the madness of theological controversies perverted by claims to final knowledge of which man is inherently incapable. Hobbes's alternative in *Leviathan* is to explicate the conditions of an order that has moral merit without dependence upon any putative *summum bonum*. He thus developed a comprehensive, powerful conception of a rule-of-law society in the full awareness of the deep-seated passions emphasized by the modern critics of association in terms of the rule of law.

Hobbes took a position on the side of one of the two recurrent characterizations of the rule of law that are integral to discussion of the rule of law. Each speaks of a commitment to the importance of law for a well-ordered society and also to the reality of the individual as the subject of legal order. Yet they are not identical.

The first characterization defends the rule of law as a necessary condition of the quest for virtuous existence in conformity with the good. Law does not define the good, in this view, but it determines the conditions of observance favorable to individuals who seek the good: individuals who bind themselves to a cooperative venture to enact good within the limits of the human condition. These individuals must enjoy liberty in order to enact good while believing that they will discover a common understanding of good through virtuous conduct. Law supports this venture but is subordinate to it, as any law that detracted from the apprehension of the good as the guide to virtuous conduct would be suspect.

The second characterization expresses skepticism that human beings can apprehend the good in a commonly agreed way. The rule of law is understood as a formal-procedural arrangement that does not elevate, promote, or defend any particular conception of good. The variety of satisfactions human beings imagine to be desirable precludes the use of law to promote or discourage particular versions of fulfillment. Rather, law is an instrumentality indicating a virtue compatible with many different goods. Law maximizes the liberty of individuals to develop their lives as they see fit. Conformity to good cannot be a matter of legal obligation: legal obligations are limited to those that are unavoidably necessary to maintain public coherence. Law does not primarily specify people's actions, nor does it provide them with advice on how to succeed in their chosen enterprises. Instead, law is an enabling device, specifying adverbial conditions or considerations that establish forms of conduct in the otherwise freely chosen pursuits of a life of self-determination. Adherence to these formalities is a virtuous achievement. A civil authority is required to determine legal obligations but not to rule on the goods people pursue. Authority is necessary to order life among individuals for whom there is little prospect of agreement with respect to goods.

Each of these two recurrent characterizations of the rule of law questions the other despite their common defense of law and individuality. The first insists that unless virtuous conduct is connected to good, virtuousness will appear empty, compatible with the trivial and the vulgar, tending to a mockery of liberty. This argument is challenged to secure willing rejection of skepticism about what is good. The very notions trivial and vulgar presuppose the availability of an objective account of good against which specific human undertakings can be judged. If the choice is between moral vulgarization and moral dogmatism, it is not surprising that many are undecided about the nature of their commitment to the rule of law.

How is it that modern political life seems to rekindle tensions that it has equally sought to relieve or dissolve? One must acknowledge a continuing, if residual, presence of the ancient understanding that modern politics has tried to supersede. This residue poses the question whether a civilization may advance scientifically while declining spiritually. The separation of politics from religion, for example, has produced desperate efforts to make politics a source of religious experience so that instead of making both politics and religion more thoughtful, both are degraded into caricature.

Efforts to articulate common understanding seem to reach an impasse when political orders seek self-sufficiency but remain uneasy in the plurality of orders. Pretensions of states to self-sufficiency seem problematic when persistence in history is not by itself enough to certify an order. It needs to be determined how that order can be properly symbolized, how one's own experience stands in relation to the myriad alternatives in the world, and what the source of the political authority is. The attempt to allay these anxieties diverts attention from the good of laws to their formal attributes, in the belief that laws of proper form can command the assent of individuals not deluded about the natural condition of mankind. Expertise is not needed to appreciate the simple advantages of peace and contentment.

Although all of this might be related in a rational account, the crucial separation of civic virtue from the quest for good requires a difficult self-transformation. The meaning of life as a public issue does not disappear. The peaceful unification of civil association is only intermittently achieved. An unending dialogue on law and its function is dignified by a kind of virtuous indecision within the liberal tradition.

Dissatisfaction with this virtuous indecision could take the form of efforts to create unity by abandoning the formality of the rule of law. The temptation to undertake such efforts is great given that the foundation of commitment to the rule of law lies in the intellectual grasp of its value against our passionate desires.

Hobbes believed in the rule of law.[1] He thought it compatible with, indeed essential to, a world in which radical skepticism about definitions of the good and man's ultimate end would prevail. Virtuous conduct would have to rest on some other foundation than agreement on the good. Among such virtues as could be known even in the state of nature is honor. Honor is manifest in those who seek glory in or take pride in the refusal to break promises or to act irrationally (without limit).

Where there is no rule of law men live by spoliation. Hobbes calls this a natural trade through which prestige is sought by material acquisition. But according to Hobbes the acquisition of prestige through spoliation permits a law of honor to "abstain from cruelty, leaving to men their lives, and instruments of husbandry."[2] He goes on to say, "Thus much the law of nature commandeth in war: that men satiate not the cruelty of their present passions, whereby in their own conscience foresee no benefit to come. For that betrayeth not a necessity, but a disposition of the mind to war, which is against the law of nature."[3]

In the conditions of nature and war, honor is a high virtue because it leads to self-limitation. In peace and society, the highest virtues are equity and justice, "and equity, justice, and honour, contain all virtues whatsoever."[4] It is evident, however, that the effects of partiality, pride, and revenge interfere with the law of honor. Honorable conduct in nature largely means refusing to break promises to oneself, but it points to something better.

The self-imposed restraint of the man of honor does not constitute acknowledgement of equality with others. But coupled with recognition of the rationality of seeking peace, it promotes the possibility of civil equality as the moral achievement of the naturally unequal.

Hobbes calls this the "relish of justice," the justice of manners in those noble or gallant few who scorn deception. The gallant few need not think of submission to the rule of law as dependency or oppression. Their subscription to law is reasonable, and they are not motivated merely by fear. They are not law-abiding for base reasons. They are neither so pretentious nor so insecure as to claim that the law robs them of authentic

felicity. Enjoying inner strength, they break the cycle in which
pretension and fear reinforce each other.

This is not inconsistent with Hobbes' assertion of natural
equality. The primary bases Hobbes advances in defense of natural equality are, first, men's equal capacity to kill each other,
and, second, each man's tendency to assume that his own share
of wisdom and insight is as good as anyone else's (i.e., that there
is no naturally acknowledged authority.)[5] At best, natural equality is a preliminary condition immediately giving rise to differences of success in attaining chosen ends.

The equal capacity to kill undermines the foundations of
self-esteem. The need to maintain self-respect imposes a competitive logic overriding temptations to be content. Natural
equality and insecurity are compatible with inequality in out-
comes and with differences in individual motivations:[6]

> The force of words, being, as I have formerly noted,
> too weak to hold men to the performance of their
> covenants; there are but two imaginable helps to
> strengthen it. And those are either a fear of the con-
> sequence of breaking their word; or a glory, or pride
> in appearing not to need to break it. This latter is a
> generosity too rarely to be found to be presumed on,
> especially in the pursuers of wealth, command, or
> sensual pleasure; which are the greatest part of man-
> kind. The passion to be reckoned upon, is fear.[7]

> That which gives to human actions the relish of jus-
> tice, is a certain nobleness or gallantness of courage,
> rarely found, by which a man scorns to be beholden
> for the contentment of his life, to fraud, or breach of
> promise. This justice of the manners, is that which
> is meant, where justice is called a virtue; and injustice
> a vice.[8]

Honor is not a motive to equality but, coupled with the
rational determination to seek peace, it promotes self-restraint
that extends to promise-keeping in covenants. The pride of the
strong in exercising self-restraint is not an acknowledgement of

equal merit. The weak therefore must invoke the vulnerability to death as the last refuge of fleeting equality. Consider Hobbes's description of the situation:

> The weakest has strength enough to kill the strongest, either by secret machination, or by confederacy with others, that are in the same danger as himself.[9]

> For nothing but fear can justify the taking away of another's life. And because fear can hardly be made manifest, but by some action dishonourable, that betrayeth the conscience of one's own weakness; all men in whom the passion of courage or magnanimity have been predominated, have abstained from cruelty; insomuch that though there be in war no law, the breach whereof is injury, yet there are those laws, the breach whereof is dishonour.[10]

The terms *confederacy* and *secret machination* are meant to contrast dishonor or desperation to the strength of keeping one's powers in reserve. Nature does not compel equality. It teaches us that we ought to want it. "Considered in mere nature," men "*ought* to admit amongst themselves equality; and he that claimeth no more, may be esteemed moderate."[11]

The rational necessity to be moderate is common to the strong and to the weak. The motives to enact such moderation differ between them. The resulting commonwealth cannot exalt one motive over the other, but it need not deny that differences exist. The rule of law presides over persons identified in terms of their civil relationship, not their natural character. To emphasize differences would mean that the transition from nature was incomplete, the mutual suspicions of the warlike tract of time remained, and the will to live civilly remained irresolute.

The strong must have the capacity to transform the virtue of honor into the virtues of equality and justice: "men *among themselves* are equal," but the temperate man "permits as much to others as he assumes to himself"; he "rightly values his power."[12] Rightly valuing one's power does not mean to Hobbes that all purposes are equally admirable. He distinguishes the admirability of a pursuit from the effort to impose it on others. We denounce "vain glory" not because all goods are relative, but because we shun "the false esteem" of our strength.[13]

Hobbes thought himself surrounded by men incompletely transformed in their self-understanding and hence living in the simulacrum of political order. The "general inclination of all mankind" is the desire for power after power, and "the cause of this, is not always that a man hopes for a more intensive delight, than he has already attained to; or that he cannot be content with a moderate power: but because he cannot assure the power and means to live well, which he hath present, without the acquisition of more."[14] Hobbes's writings continually point out the difference between the untransformed natural and the transformed civil attitude. Just and unjust persons are distinguished according to the different motives behind their externally just actions. In practice, the relation of motive to action is ambiguous, but the point of the distinction is evident enough.

> for the unjust man who abstaineth from injuries for fear of punishment, declareth plainly that the justice of his actions dependeth upon civil constitution, from whence punishments proceed; which would otherwise in the estate of nature be unjust, according to the fountain from whence they spring.[15]

> When injustice is taken for guilt, the action is unjust, but not therefore the man; and when justice is taken for guiltlessness, the actions are just, and yet not always the man.[16]

Guilt and guiltlessness are civil findings in the rule of law, only formally precluding judgments of character. But since "for peace sake, nature hath ordained this law, *That every man acknowledge other for his equal*,"[17] judgments of character must be restrained in favor of determinations of guilt and guiltlessness. Despite the reasons to differentiate one man from another, then, there are powerful motives to accept civil equality. One such motive for the strong lies in disdaining the appearance of needing

to attain self-esteem through domination. To resist this temptation helps to avoid the absurdity of refusing to will peace.
There is a less admirable (in that respect weaker) motive based
in fear.

Strength of character would also show itself in disdaining
envy. A man should not "study so much his neighbor's profits
as his own," nor should he "divide his goods amongst his neighbors," but "he should esteem his neighbor worthy all rights and
privileges that he himself enjoyeth; and attribute unto him, whatsoever he looketh should be attributed to himself."[18] That is,
one wills to see others not as natural competitors but as fellow
subjects in the civil order.

The attractiveness of such accommodation derives from
the strength of the commitment to the project of creatively ordering and disciplining the inner flow of experience. One vis-
ualizes a self-sufficient individual discovering a world of
significance that would excite the envy of others if they knew
the full extent of its possibilities and puzzles. And these excite-
ments, which were perhaps dimly intuited by the powerful in
the natural condition, open up new worlds to conquer and ho-
rizons to explore without need of robbery, spoliation, or con-
firmation from the multitude. This is the true doctrine of the
moral individualist.

The rule of law can have special appeal to the strongest
individuals if they are not passionate merely to overpower
the weak, and if they see that there is far more to seek than
wealth, command, or sensual delight. It is doubtful that all
will appreciate this, but self-restraint for the sake of broaden-
ing self-exploration can be greeted with enthusiasm by the
inwardly strong. In the refusal to elevate any particular pursuit, the rule of law supports the individual's dependence on
his own strength of character.

The general desire for peace and a contented life, however,
goes with fear of failure, submission, and death in support of a
sovereign and the rule of law. In not elevating any pursuit, the
rule of law protects the fearful. Impartiality lies in the indifference
of law to pursuits. The drama of evaluation is a private, interior

dialogue of the self. The strong individual's satisfaction coincides with this dedramatization of the public realm.

Hobbes mediates the divine and the civil by eliminating the necessity of a collective symbolization of the eternal and the temporal. Hobbes clearly feared the inclination to make immanent and politicize the idea of a divine destiny. He saw the religious motive as a pretext for revolutionary violence. De-emphasizing religion was then a sign of respect for the power of religious experience, and it suggests a desire to avoid its easy perversion in political life.

Hobbes analyzed the psychology of religious zeal to demystify inspired disputes. By eliminating madness or possession, he meant to dissuade men from the belief that the natural laws give access to God's purposes, rationalizing their rebelliousness. Neither rulers nor multitudes should be permitted such extravagance:

> There be some that proceed further; and will not have the law of nature, to be those rules which conduce to the preservation of man's life on earth; but to the attaining of an eternal felicity after death; to which they think the breach of covenant may conduce; and consequently be just and reasonable; such are they that think it a work of merit to kill, or depose, or rebel against, the sovereign power constituted over them by their own consent. But because there is no natural knowledge of man's estate after death; much less of the reward that is then to be given to breach of faith; but only a belief grounded upon other men's saying, that they know it supernaturally, or that they know those, that knew them, that knew others, that knew it supernaturally; breach of faith cannot be called a precept of reason, or nature.[19]

As the man of honor translates self-restraint in nature into law-abidingness in civil society, so he maintains the distinction between earthly peace and the mysteries of human existence. Earthly eloquence is not a guarantee of insight into divine purpose; perhaps it is a blasphemy. These reflections, however, cannot guarantee that self-regulation will prevail. There is much to seduce one away from self-regulation. Those who incite the multitude by claiming possession of a spirit are not true prophets:

> For neither Moses nor Abraham pretended to proph-
> ecy by possession of a spirit; but from the voice of
> God; or by a vision or a dream: nor is there anything
> in his law, moral or ceremonial, by which they were
> taught, there was any such enthusiasm, or any pos-
> session. . . . The Scriptures, by the Spirit of God in
> man, mean a man's spirit, inclined to godli-
> ness. . . . Neither did the other prophets of the Old
> Testament pretend enthusiasm; or; that God spake in
> them; but to them, by voice, vision, or dream; and
> the *burthen of the Lord* was not possession, but com-
> mand. How then could the Jews fall into this opinion
> of possession? I can imagine no reason, but that which
> is common to all men, namely, the want of curiosity
> to search natural causes. . . . The Scripture was writ-
> ten to shew unto men the kingdom of God, and to
> prepare their minds to become his obedient subjects;
> leaving the world, and the philosophy thereof to the
> disputation of men, for the exercising of their natural
> reason.[20]

Self-regulation is in constant danger of being overwhelmed by self-forgetfulness. On the one hand, the peace and unity of a commonwealth connect enforceable laws with freedom for self-exploration and they prepare the mind to become God's obedient subject. On the other hand, there is a temptation to forget the self in the seditious roaring of the mob incited by eloquence.

This polarity is not easily disposed of. Self-regulation is not given to us; we must give it to ourselves. There is, however, potential nobility in self-regulation even though it is not a nobility of display. It is a greater achievement than overpowering or submitting to others. One can accommodate others in order to be freed from the mundane forms of pursuing wealth, command, or sensuous delight.

The covenant is Hobbes's symbol for the transformation

in the individual who, by following Hobbes's teaching would be empowered to unify his life. The unity would consist in seeking the means to realize self-chosen purposes without requiring social legitimation. For the man of honor this means a transformation of the law of honor by submitting without complaint to the rule of law. For the weak, the change is symbolized in the obvious comparison of war to peace and contentment. Both would then say, "when a man hath . . . abandoned, or granted away his right; then he is said to be obligated, or bound, not to hinder those to whom such a right is granted, or abandoned, from the benefit of it."[21]

For "it is against reason for a knowing man to do a thing in vain."[22] So long as one deliberates on these matters, one has not willed the transformation. But to will it is to conclude one's deliberations. Is the will to covenant irrevocable? By nature, it is not. In logic, it is. To say one ought to covenant is to say one must. A covenant issues from promises that are made in certainty of mutual benefit, and it is understood that the liberty to perform or not perform "is taken away" and the promises "consequently are obligatory".[23] And "a promise is equivalent to a covenant."[24]

Hobbes assumes that the intention of speakers is to make others understand them.[25] Potential associates in covenant must assume this, but they also cannot help appraising each other because, by nature if not in reason, deception is an everpresent temptation. The unavoidable natural condition of mankind is to experience the tension of the universal, equal predicament of seeking felicity while fending off misery: every covenanter is simultaneously a covenantee. Natural conditions promote self-restraint, although they do not determine it a necessary or automatic process.

The tension between nature and reason in experience makes possible man's moral achievement in the civil order without reducing it to a mechanical, submoral fact. When one lays down the natural right to do X, one acquires an obligation not to do X. This formality does not explain how such obligations actually come into being.

One knows that one ought not do X, but one can also

believe that one could get away with *X*. Man imposes restraint
on natural liberty in order to gain civil (civilized) liberty. The
restraint is artificial in that it is an artifact, something made by
man, not by natural processes. Man is, Hobbes says, both the
matter to be formed and the maker that forms the matter.[26]

Artifices reflect self-chosen purposes. Man wants to liberate
himself from being moved only by the contingencies of passion
in order to be moved within self-imposed boundaries. These
boundaries enhance the capacity to act for the long term and not
according to immediate necessities.

The binding nature of the covenant derives not from nature
but from reason. By the logic of the covenant the individual is
bound because self-bound, and a rational individual does not
want to act absurdly, which is not to say that circumstance will
never impose absurdity on him.[27]

Where there is no covenant (conversation) there can be no
injury (absurdity). The law of honor is not covenant since there
is no promise except by the strong to themselves: violation of
the law of honor is a matter of personal interpretation. What
may appear to another to be absurd or injurious is beside the
point.

Hobbes's man has no illusions about his vulnerability,
however wise or talented he may be, and he will also shun
inconsistency, self-contradiction, and the erratic. Nature urges
him to self-awareness, reason to self-respect. Reason exalts
where nature humbles.

The balance of reason and nature yields the self-restrained
man. There arises a detached perspective on the claim to wisdom
that need not exclude the possibility that wisdom can be sought.
The fool says there is neither justice nor God; the self-restrained
man says no such things.[28] To know there is no God is not
possible for man, but it is reasonable to conclude that there is
no unarguable interpretation of what the word *God* signifies:
"there are no wars so sharply waged as between sects of the
same religion."[29]

In order to covenant we must bind ourselves. The threat of
punishment for noncompliance follows the convenant, it does

not precede it. Obligation to the law must rely on the will of each to observe it. In this prospect lies the hope of peace, contentment, and eliminating reliance upon standing armies.

The honorable and the fearful are both capable of rational response to the natural condition of mankind. The circumstances of each give rise to different passions, but the logic of covenant produces a common result for all—that is justice—and it does so by enabling authority to voice the law for all because it speaks for no one in particular.

The possibility of authority depends on the prior, inner transformation of the individual through the covenant. Rationality is common even if bodies and their movements are irreducibly individual. It is the continued tension between private motives and common reason that allows the covenant to be Hobbes's ultimate symbol of the self-transforming capacity in man. The covenant is not, finally, a unique event but the paradigm of a lifetime of rational willing, the test of the enduring capacity for self-overcoming in civil association.

Notes

1. *Leviathan*, ed. by Michael Oakeshott (New York: Blackwell, 1960): chap. 14, p. 92; chap. 16, p. 108; chap. 21, pp. 143–44; chap. 26, p. 184; chap. 27, p. 192. Hereafter cited as *Lev*.
2. *Lev*, chap. 17, p. 109.
3. *The Elements of Law Natural and Politic*, ed. by Ferdinand Tonnies (New York: Cambridge University Press, 1928): part I, chap. 19.2, p. 78. Hereafter this edition will be referred to as *EL*.
4. *EL*, chap. 17.15, p. 73.
5. *Lev*, chap. 13, p. 80.
6. *Lev*, chap. 13, p. 81.
7. *Lev*, chap. 14, p. 92.
8. *Lev*, chap. 15, p. 97.
9. *Lev*, chap. 13, p. 80.
10. *EL*, chap. 19.2, p. 78.
11. *EL*, chap. 14.2, p. 54. My italics.
12. *The Citizens*, ed. by Bernard Gert. (Garden City: Anchor Books,

1972): p. 114. Hereafter this edition will be referred to as *TC*. My italics.

13. *TC*, p. 114.

14. *Lev*, chap. 11, p. 64.

15. *EL*, chap. 16.10, p. 64. *EL*, chap. 16.10, pp. 66–67. Moreover, "And seeing the laws of nature concern the conscience, not he only breaketh them that doth any action contrary but also he whose action is comformable to them in case he think it despiseth the law" (*EL*, chap. 17.13, p. 72). When action and judgment are consistent with each other, and consistently aimed toward our preservation in peace through moderation, then we have a virtuous habit (*EL*, chap. 17.14, p. 73 and *Lev*, chap. 15, p. 97).

16. *Ibid*.

17. *EL*, chap. 17.1, pp. 68–69.

18. *EL*, chap. 18.6, p. 75.

19. *Lev*, chap. 15, p. 96.

20. *Lev*, chap. 8, pp. 49–50.

21. *Lev*, chap. 14, p. 86.

22. *TC*, p. 136.

23. *EL*, chap. 15.9, p. 60.

24. *Lev*, chap. 14, p. 88.

25. *EL*, chap. 13.10, p. 53.

26. *Lev*, Introduction, p. 5; chap. 29, p. 210.

27. "There is a great similitude between that we call injury, or injustice in the actions and conversations of men in the world, and that which is called *absurd* in the arguments and disputations of the Schools. For as he, that is driven to contradict an assertion by him before maintained, is said to be reduced to an absurdity; so he that through passion doth, or omitteth that which before by covenant he promised not to do, or not to omit, is said to commit injustice. And there is in every breach of covenant a contradiction properly so called . . . he that violateth a covenant, willeth the doing of the same thing, at the same time . . . injury is an absurdity of conversation, as absurdity is a kind of injustice in disputation" (*EL*, chap. 16.2, pp. 63–64).

28. *Lev*, chap. 15, pp. 94–95.

29. *TC*, p. 114.

DAVID
LOWENTHAL

VII

Locke on Conquest

Despite claims from the left, liberalism and the republics founded on it are inherently peace-loving. Liberal republics have little taste for war as such and none for massive wars of conquest, though they have been tempted into limited wars of commercial acquisition. From the beginning, their object has been to reduce and ameliorate war—which eventually led them to think of outlawing it through international organizations. Their love of peace could even become so great as to beget the mortal dangers Churchill portrays in *The Gathering Storm*. It was not the love of war but the love of peace and security that made Britain and France delude themselves about Hitler. In general, liberal societies leave the strategic initiative to their enemies, and their greatest danger comes from enemies to whose real and often explicitly stated goals they refuse to give credence to. Challenged by totalitarian systems glorifying war for the sake of either race or class, their naivete and excessive devotion to peace make it difficult for them to hold their own. Liberal principles add to this difficulty by calling for a limit to armed conflict among nations.

Liberalism is the revolutionary modern system of politics built on the primacy of the individual and his inalienable rights. Its originators were two seventeenth-century English philosophers, Hobbes and Locke. According to both, war is the condition that prevails among men before they establish government, and the object of government is to establish domestic peace and justice, along with enough strength to resist foreign enemies. Of war's several causes, says Hobbes, one of the foremost is the love of glory and superiority most often found in aristocratic monarchies or republics. This martial spirit is the source of needless bloodshed abroad and oppressive and unproductive rule at home. Another source of war is competition for scarce resources. In fact, so pervasive did Hobbes think the causes of war, prior to government, that he considered the war of all against all man's natural condition. But men also have a natural and absolute right to self-preservation, and the first dictate of human reason, the "first law of nature" (*Leviathan*, chap. XIV), is to seek peace. The means of securing peace is government—inherently a sovereign and mighty Leviathan, but a Leviathan sorely weakened until now. Not only have its inherent powers been misunderstood, but is has also been crippled by false notions of glory and religion that cause men to undervalue its products—life and peace on earth. Strengthened now by Hobbes's denigration of both aristocracy and Christianity, government can provide the conditions necessary for self-preservation and a comfortable life. It can encourage the individual's peaceable production of wealth and excite terror in the unjust. Thus the mighty Leviathan builds a secure enclave for its subjects, even as the state of nature continues among the Leviathans themselves.

After all this emphasis on war as the evil most to be avoided, it is remarkable how little attention Hobbes gives problems of foreign policy. "Peace and defense" are the true objects of government, yet the "right of making war, and peace with other nations" is listed as only the ninth of twelve rights of sovereignty (*Leviathan*, chap. XVIII) and as the last of the offices or duties of the sovereign (chap. XXX). While the sovereign has the right and duty, by the law of nature and nations, to procure the safety of his people Hobbes explains that "by safety here, is not meant a bare Preservation, but also all other Contentments of life, which every man by lawful industry, without danger or hurt to the Commonwealth, shall acquire to himself" (chap. XXX). In the chapter on the "Nutrition and Procreation of a Commonwealth" (chap. XXIV) he suggests that wars for planting colonies of the poor and for acquiring not only necessities but contentments can be justified. Later (in reference to colonization), Hobbes forbids the extermination of peoples na-

tive to countries "not sufficiently inhabited," but he sanctions
forcing them to farm small plots of land in place of hunting or
grazing over a wide territory (chap. XXX). Nations, therefore,
are not strictly limited to wars of self-preservation. Nevertheless,
commonwealths founded on a Hobbesian basis will clearly have
a civil or civilian, that is, a mercantile, orientation rather than a
military one. The commonwealth is not attracted to wars of
conquest for ambition's sake, nor does it encourage deeds of
glory, the risking of life, or even the military as an occupation.
Defense is its primary focus, and only in the name of defense—
especially when the nation is under direct attack—does the "help
of all that are able to bear arms" become obligatory (chap. XXI).

While the essential features of sovereignty are always the
same, Hobbes distinguishes between two forms of commonwealth, depending on how they were brought about. The first
is commonwealth by institution, in which men voluntarily set
a sovereign over themselves out of mutual fear. The second—
commonwealth by acquisition—occurs when sovereignty is not
voluntarily chosen but compelled, and shows itself in either conquest or in the family. Hobbes uses the word *dominion* rather
than *commonwealth* to embrace these forms of sovereignty by
acquisition, perhaps because the word "commonwealth" seems
inappropriate to the family. The natural dominion of father or
parents over children presumes consent on the part of children,
out of fear, to rulers they have not chosen. It is acquired by
generation but depends essentially on the child's consent. In
discussing the family (chap. XX), Hobbes elevates the natural
right of the mother to a plane of equality with that of the father,
in effect equalizing the sexes and striking still another blow at
the role of masculinity and the martial spirit in human affairs.
Thus the notion of sexual equality enters liberal thought at its
very origin.

The second kind of dominion, or commonwealth by acquisition, comes from conquest. Hobbes calls it despotical, and
describes it as the rule of lords or masters over consenting servants. It derives from the fear of the vanquished that they will
be killed if they fail to serve the victor. But servants are not

slaves: they are entrusted with their "corporal liberty" (*Levi-athan*, ch. XX), whereas slaves are kept in chains or prisons and never enter into a state of obligation to their masters. The question of the justness of conquest never arises for Hobbes: there is neither just nor unjust in the state of nature prevailing among sovereign powers. Moreover, Hobbes insists that sovereignty involved in commonwealth by institution and commonwealth by acquisition are both based on fear, are equally legitimate, and involve identical powers. It follows that the rights of the victors and duties of the vanquished remain the same in all conquests. Thus, a conquered people owes unending and complete fidelity to its conquerors and sovereigns, to whom they are related as servant to master. The consequence is a serious and apparent inadequacy, if not an outright inconsistency, in Hobbes's teaching on war. Nations, like individuals, have a right to make war necessary for self-preservation (which can be extended to include the comfortable life): only such wars have a just intention. Yet, since justice has no place in the state of nature, no war can be called just or unjust. All successful conquests, therefore, obligate the vanquished (other than those enslaved) to the same unending obedience. And this obedience is no different from that owed by someone who has freely chosen his own sovereign.

Locke tries to make Hobbes's philosophy more consistent by bringing it closer in some ways to moral common sense, although he also introduces daring innovations. At first he portrays man's natural condition as one of peace, only occasionally disrupted by conflict (*Second Treatise of Civil Government*, chap. 2). Later, for no apparent reason, the state of nature is shown to be or to have grown exceedingly insecure—hardly different from a war of all against all (sec. 123). It is at this point that political societies or commonwealths, ruled by governments, become urgently necessary. Their object is to make and enforce laws for the protection of the God-given rights of their members to life, liberty, and property. They are "to employ the force of the community at home only in the execution of such laws, or abroad to prevent or redress foreign injuries, and secure the community from inroads and invasion. And all this to be directed to no other end but the peace, safety, and public good of the people" (sec. 131). Even more stringently than in Hobbes, the object of foreign affairs is limited to self-defense. But in giving almost all his attention to the internal composition and business of political societies rather than to the conduct of foreign affairs and war, Locke seems to differ little from Hobbes. The federative power—one of three fundamental powers in every common-wealth—receives only the briefest treatment, despite its involving the power of "war and peace, leagues and alliances, and all the transactions with all persons and communities without the commonwealth" (sec. 146).

Through much of the first half of the *Second Treatise* the reader senses a preoccupation with the problem of war. Locke claims that "the governments of the world that were begun in peace" had their origin in popular consent (sec. 104). But the paucity of his historical examples demonstrates that few were so begun: most were begun in war. In chapter XVI, Locke turns from consent as the only legitimate source of political authority to the claims made for force—that is, to the role of ambition, the "noise of war," and the claim of those (like Hobbes) who reckon "conquest as one of the originals of government" (sec. 175). Earlier, in chapter VI, Locke takes paternal (or parental) power out from under the Hobbesian rubric of dominion by acquisition. The last chapters are devoted to the internal breakdown of governments through the onset of tyranny. But in chapter XVI Locke pays the closest attention to Hobbes's political alternative to commonwealth by institution or consent—dominion by conquest.

Chapter XVI has one simple point: some wars are just and some unjust (reintroducing a traditional distinction), but conquest is never justified. This was an astonishingly new idea. With this sweeping contradiction of Hobbes, Locke lays the basis for thought on war that became the common sense of twentieth-century liberal societies. The concepts of aggressor nations, reparations, wars of national liberation and national self-determination are all here in this chapter. Against the successful conquest by an aggressor, according to Locke, there exists an enduring right on the part of the conquered people to liberate themselves. But the much more difficult case—and hence more extensively treated—is that of the "conqueror in a lawful war" (sec. 177): what power does he get, and over whom? If one nation is unjustly attacked by another, what right of conquest does the victim have against its attacker?

Such a defensive conqueror "gets no power but only over those who have actually assisted, concurred, or consented to that unjust force that is used against him" (sec. 179). The rest are innocent and cannot be touched. In regard to those who helped attack him unjustly, he has a right over their lives but none over their possessions. This, Locke acknowledges, is a "strange doctrine," since it is "so contrary to the practice of the world." He says, "The right, then, of conquest extends only to the lives of those who joined in the war, not to their estates, but only in order to make reparation for the damages received and the charges of war, and that, too, with reservation of the right of the innocent wife and children" (sec. 182). This is the basis for the Treaty of Versailles' assignment of war guilt to Germany after World War I and for the taking of reparations by the Allies, as victims of aggression.

In and of itself Locke's doctrine can have different and even opposing practical effects. It can cause the original unjust aggressor to think more lightly of aggression, as only those directly involved in the aggression will be affected by failure. Those directly involved in the aggression, however, have every reason to fight vigorously, knowing that if they fail they will be branded as war criminals and put to the sword or enslaved. The prospect of not being harmed will also encourage all the peace elements in the aggressor society to refrain from assisting—and if possible to work against—the war effort, thus making it more difficult for unjust aggression to occur or to succeed. The innocent are reinforced in opposing their country's misdeeds, but this could compel a country bent on aggression to find ways of sweeping everyone into the war effort, perhaps through massive propaganda. Instead of a political society being considered a unit bearing responsibility for its unjust actions, as in the past, it is then considered a composite of parts: those for the war, those against the war, and those engaged in the war effort voluntarily. An additional part consists of those—women and children especially—accorded a right of survival superior to a claim of reparations by the victimized but winning nation. Applied to the conditions of all-out war, where the whole civilian population contributes to the war effort, the principle would still make possible a general retaliation.

The aggressor nation can be compelled to pay reparations, but its lands may not be seized by the victim nation. Permanent appropriation would far outweigh in value the limited damage inflicted on the victim nation. In the process of deciding reparations, the aggressor's seizure of the victim's money is not to be held against him: unlike real goods such as grain, the value of money is declared to be only conventional and imaginary (sec. 184). Again distinguishing between the practice of mankind (what has been done) and the dictates of justice (what should be done), Locke reiterates his strange conclusion that no conquest is ever justified(sec. 185, 187). The victims of aggression have every right to resist conquest and gain victory, but they themselves never receive a right to conquer. Reparations are all they can justly claim.

Locke reaffirms a double right with which every man is born: first, a right to consent to be governed and hence to leave the country in which he is born (though without his inherited possessions; second, a claim to the inheritance of his ancestors if he stays, even if conquest—just or unjust—has until then deprived him and his countrymen of that inheritance: "Who doubts but the Grecian Christians, descendants of the ancient possessors of that country, may justly cast off the Turkish yoke which they have so long groaned under, whenever they have an opportunity to do it?" (sec. 192). Here we see the origin of the appeal to nationalism and national self-determination that has become so strong since the nineteenth century—an appeal to a social bond more cohesive than common humanity and not easily squared with the differences toward national enemies encouraged above. For an idea of what Locke thought justified in his own country, replace the Turks in the passage cited above with the ruling

Normans, and the Grecian Christians with the subject populations in England (including some Normans [sec. 177]). This
shows the insufficiency of the standard view of Locke as an
apologist for the sentiments that led to the Glorious Revolution.
Locke's principles transcend the settlement of 1689, for no settlement retaining the Norman monarchy and House of Lords
could possibly satisfy them. What he wanted for England, by
implication, was a war of national liberation that would establish
a pure form of liberal representative government. In this respect,
a single practical theme bearing on England united the concluding chapters of the *Two Treatises on Government*, moving from
conquest to the final dissolution and reconstitution of government through revolution.

To gauge the overall effect of Locke's ideas on international
affairs, one must distinguish between the nations that are built
on his liberal foundations and those that are not. Lockean nations
would be reluctant to go to war unless impelled by self-preservation, and they would refrain from conquering lands and
peoples. Nations that combine being non-Lockean with being
aggressive (such as Nazi Germany and the USSR) will be helped
by the peace-loving nature of Lockean nations and will hardly
be bound by Locke's restrictions on conquest. From within they
can be impeded by peace-loving forces only if such forces are
aware of their likely immunity to harm at the end of a lost
aggressive war, and if they are permitted to exist: propaganda
and totalitarian controls reduce this possibility to a minimum.
Locke's doctrine works to undermine all settlements after conquests if they involve subjugating or keeping lands and peoples.
The more decent the conquering or imperial nation, the more
susceptible it is to nationalistic uprisings, regardless of how well
it has treated its subordinate peoples. Claims to national autonomy will prove upsetting not only to bad settlements but also
to good ones—like the Norman settlement Locke was determined to destroy, which the English have nevertheless seen fit
to preserve. These claims will shatter old empires or countries
through wars of liberation and frequently replace them with
regimes more destructive of liberty or less able to sustain their

own independence. In the USSR, for example, built on the subjugation of innumerable nationalities, these claims are forcibly
prevented from having this effect.

The very notion of aggressive war presumes an equal right
to self-preservation for all nations regardless of their internal
character. This principle can be subordinated only if a nation
retains conquered peoples and lands within its dominion. Aggressive war can be likened to the crime of assault within civil
society—except that Locke will not allow for something parallel
to life imprisonment or capital punishment in the case of the
criminal nation. At the same time that aggressive war is made
a crime—and hence worsened in its moral severity—its punishment is reined back. This makes for constant war guilt and war
crimes accusations that lead toward demands for unconditional
surrender and intensification of the conflict. Yet by setting such
limits on what can justly be done to defeated aggressor nations,
Locke forces victorious victim nations to engage in subterfuge
and hypocrisy in their peace settlements. Or, since they may not
appropriate lands and peoples, they are induced to engage in
great political experiments aimed at transforming enemies into
friends through the imposition of constitutional democracy. Germany is an example of this experiment. After fourteen years of
the Weimar Republic the transformation led to the ascendancy
of Adolf Hitler and a second world war. Even after atrocious
aggression, the Lockean West renounces its just conquests, but
the unjust conquests of Nazi Germany had to be wrested from
it by massive force, and no force is now capable of stripping
similar conquests from the USSR.

Locke's doctrine works against aggression and for peace,
but it can also work against the just and decent nations accepting
the doctrine. It makes them excessively devoted to peace in a
world of enemies, excessively respectful of the territorial integ-
rity of other nations despite their threat to peace and their own
people, and obedient to rules of conquest aggressor nations disregard. A world already filled with liberal societies would be
less harmed by Locke's doctrine, but it would also need this
doctrine less. A world in which liberal societies have to cope

with aggressive antiliberal societies would tilt toward antiliberalism because of the doctrine and the liberal ethos surrounding it. The spirited war Hobbes and Locke started against the martial spirit could then prove its own undoing. The survival of that martial spirit is necessary to the survival of liberalism itself. Was this not clear to Locke, who knew his project required the cudgeling of kings (sec. 235), and who never promised perpetual peace? Has it not in fact been the salvation of liberal societies in the great revolutions that brought them into existence and the great wars that have been fought for their survival? Was Locke wrong in supposing that a free society would be prepared to do for the sake of securing the tangible benefits of freedom what other ages have done for honor, God, nation, and country?

NATHAN
TARCOV

VIII

The Spirit of Liberty and
Early American Foreign Policy

If America's prospects in our third century depend on our for-tifying our moral resources at the spirited wells of modernity,[1] then it is necessary to question whether the American founding partakes of a spirited version of modernity. If our founding was instead informed by the demotion of spiritedness on behalf at best of peace and freedom and at worst of acquisitive self-in-dulgence, then America's prospects would seem very bleak.[2]

It is tempting to view the American dedication to the rights of life, liberty, and the pursuit of happiness and to the consent of the people, like the theories of rights and consent of Hobbes and Locke, as part of a project to purge politics of the angry element of spiritedness and reduce it to rational calculation for the satisfaction of desire. Such a project would stand in contrast to the sobriety and moderation of the Platonic recognition of the necessary and central political role of spiritedness as the sup-port of justice and the ally of reason against desire.

The Lockean theory of rights and consent, at least, seems to rest on a more complicated political psychology, including a significant positive political role for spiritedness. For Locke, at least, the assertion of rights is more than a mere expression of desires or preferences; it is a spirited claim that there are duties both to respect other's rights and to vindicate one's own rights. Whereas Hobbes could reckon on fear as the passion conducive to obedience, Locke hoped to inspire dangerous resistance to governments that endanger rights as well as safe obedience to those that secure rights. Accordingly, the body of the *Two Trea-tises* opens with an appeal to a spirited disdain for slavery:

> Slavery is so vile and miserable an Estate of Man, and so directly opposite to the generous Temper and Courage of our Nation; that 'tis hardly to be con-ceived, that an *Englishman*, much less a *Gentleman*, should plead for't.[3]

Although the jural argument of the *Two Treatises*—for a right to kill others in order to protect one's right to liberty—depends on regarding liberty as "the Fence" . . . necessary to and closely joyned with a Man's Preservation,"[4] the hortatory appeal to exercise that right, at the risk of one's own life, depends on regarding liberty as more than an instrument of comfortable preservation. In this way Locke may be said to have laid the groundwork for the idealist "philosophy of freedom."[5] This generous temper and courage is the positive side of the phenom-enon understood by classical political philosophy as *thymos* or spiritedness.[6]

In the jural argument of the *Two Treatises* the connection of liberty to preservation entitles one to kill others in order to protect one's liberty. This connection also prevents one from forfeiting liberty except by acts that forfeit one's life.[7] According to Locke, the connection of liberty to rationality entitles one to liberty in the first place, as "we are *born Free*, as we are born Rational" in the sense that "the *Freedom* then of Man and Liberty of acting according to his own Will, is *grounded on* his having *Reason*."[8] Men are by nature free because they are by nature rational. Yet Locke also argues more broadly that "Man has a *Natural Freedom* . . . since all that share in the common Nature, Faculties and Power, are in Nature equal."[9] Locke's hortatory argument is indeed occasionally stated as if aspects of human nature other than rationality may entitle those who possess them to liberty. He sarcastically says that conquerors have a "Right of Principality . . . to have their Yoke cast off, as soon as God shall give those under their subjection Courage and Opportunity to do it,"[10] as if courage or the will to defend one's liberty when one has the chance were what entitled men to liberty. Similarly, Locke defends the right of resistance against "servile Flatterers, who whilst it seem'd to serve their turn, resolv'd all Government into absolute Tyranny, and would have all Men born to, what their mean Souls fitted them for, Slavery."[11] He thus argues almost as if servility of soul rather than the violation of the rights of others condemned men to slavery, while liberality of soul rather than rationality would entitle men to be free, and therefore not all men were born to freedom. Thus the final argument of the work, like the opening, appeals to the English gentleman's love of liberty and disdain for slavery. The *Two Treatises*, however, is primarily a jural work concerned with the rights and duties of men under the law of nature. Its emphasis therefore is on the foundation of the right to liberty in preservation and rationality. The love of liberty, on which the work's persuasive power rests, is marginal to the primary argument.

The spirited love of liberty and disdain for slavery are a major concern of Locke's *Some Thoughts Concerning Education*, directed primarily to the English gentry.[12] Aspects of that work may at first suggest an alliance of reason and desire against spiritedness. The education Locke offers is thus directed in large part against the love of dominion. It is based on the premises that the happiness all men pursue consists in pleasure; that the preservation of all mankind as much as in him lies is everyone's duty and "the true Principle to regulate our Religion, Politicks and Morality by"; that self-preservation disposes us to hearken to reason, while fear is a monitor to quicken our industry; and that "where there is no Desire, there will be no Industry."[13] *Some Thoughts Concerning Education* and the *Two Treatises* thus both defend the industrious and rational and their property against the quarrelsome and contentious. Locke here too is providing against "the Natural Vanity and Ambition of Men, too apt of it self to grow and encrease with the Possession of any Power." This vanity and ambition includes both "the Ambition or Insolence of Empire" and "the Pride, Ambition, and Turbulency of private Men."[14] Locke's opposition, however, still leaves room for a positive role for properly educated spiritedness.

The fundamental psychological basis for morality in Locke's *Thoughts* is neither physical fear nor sensual desire, but pride in one's liberty and rationality. Locke observes that "We would be thought Rational Creatures, and have our Freedom"; men have "a Mind to shew that they are free, that their own good Actions come from themselves, that they are absolute and independent." He claims that children share these basic tendencies with adults.[15] Since human beings love liberty and resent duty,[16] human nature supports a pedagogy, a morality, and a politics of rights and liberty rather than of duties and imposition. Liberty, for Locke, is based not so much on rationality as on pride in liberty and rationality. This pride in liberty is possible because human beings can love liberty more than the particular object of desire owing to the indefiniteness of human desire. There are no innate ideas of particular objects, only indefinite desires for pleasure and for avoidance of pain either directed by experience to particular objects or left less definite as desires for liberty, variety, and esteem.[17]

In Locke's *Thoughts,* the complexity of spiritedness is indicated by the relation between those aspects that suggest an alliance of reason and desire against the spirited love of dominion and those that reveal a reliance on the spirited love of liberty. The love of dominion Locke's education opposes and the love of liberty it favors are indeed the two sides of what Locke calls *pride.* No other creatures, he notes, "are half so wilful and proud, or half so desirous to be Masters of themselves and others, as Man."[18] Human pride is a love of both liberty and dominion, both self-mastery and mastery over others.[19] Locke attempts to control the proud desire for mastery over others by satisfying the proud desire for liberty and mastery over oneself. The desire for mastery is turned inward against one's own passions. Effecting this depends on both self-denial (an acquired ability based on the natural ability to suspend one's desires)[20] and the partly natural and partly nurtured love of reputation or esteem.[21] The tyrannical desire for gaining mastery over others must give way to the civil desire for winning esteem in order to make human nature safe for liberal, civil society. The desire to be treated as a rational creature and to show one is free is social in a way that merely sensual desires are not. This desire points toward a recognition of the liberty and rationality of others as the conditions of the recognition of one's own—a virtuous relation of esteem and civility instead of a vicious circle of tyranny and slavery.

Locke seems to have judged it safer to discourage the spirited inclination toward dominion by encouraging the spirited concern for liberty, esteem, and self-mastery, than to overcome spiritedness altogether by relying simply on fear and sensual desire. His policies of liberty, toleration, and resistance depend on the capacity of men to express their pride and spirit by insisting on rights without tyrannizing over others.[22] In the *Thoughts*, Locke states that it is the great art and true secret of education to steer between the Scylla of inability to master one's inclinations, caused by excessive indulgence of desire, and the Charybdis of "*dejected Minds*, timorous and tame, and *low Spirits*" caused by excessive imposition of fear.[23] Between these extremes, Locke seeks "to keep up a Child's Spirit, easy, active and free," neither a "low spirited" and "*Slavish Temper*" nor a disorderly one.[24] Ultimately, the connection of spiritedness and rationality through pride shapes spiritedness to the needs of a liberal society.

The American founding, at least in its Lockean source, therefore rests on an appreciation of the positive as well as the negative political potential of spiritedness. It remains to investigate that theme within the founding and early existence of the American republic itself.

What could be more quintessentially spirited than a declaration of independence?[25] The most fundamental document of the American founding does not, however, assume a separate and equal station for the American people simply out of the spirited desire for self-mastery. This spirited assumption of a free and independent status is presented first of all as a "necessary" act, an alteration to which 'necessity . . . constrains them." They merely "acquiesce in the necessity," a posture apparently distinct from spirited self-assertion.[26] The necessity involved, however, is neither physical nor historical but moral: it is the necessity of exercising a right or fulfilling a duty. The Declaration claims that it is a right or a duty on the part of a people to overthrow a government that "evinces a design to reduce them under absolute despotism" or to establish "an absolute tyranny" over them. Exercising this right in defense of all one's rights is a spirited as well as a moral act. It is an act of self-defense and vindication rather than the mere expression of anger, vindictiveness, or the desire for mastery.

The Declaration has the implicit requirement that the right of the people to alter or abolish their form of government and assume independence can be exercised only when necessary. This is a rationalization and moralization of spiritedness which has several important implications. First, the Declaration is more than an act of self-assertion as an assumption of independence and a declaration by a people of their own rights. It implies respect for the sources of those rights in nature and nature's God and respect for others, who have the same rights, including that "decent respect to the opinions of mankind" that requires the Declaration not merely of independence but of the causes impelling Americans to independence. Second, the Declaration does not claim, as mere spiritedness might, that it is the duty or even necessarily the right of every dependent people to assume an independent status. On the contrary, it implies the legitimacy of the political connection between the American people and Great Britain up until the point at which its dissolution became necessary. Similarly, it does not claim that it is the duty or even necessarily the right of every people under a monarchy or even under a defective form of government to alter it. The Declaration complains not that the British empire was a monarchy or even one that permitted abuses, but that George III actually committed "every act which may define a tyrant." Both the assumption of independence and the alteration of a form of government depend on the prior violation of rights and the danger of their future elimination—despotism or tyranny. The Declaration, therefore, third, leaves room for prudence to judge whether violations of rights constitute mere light and transient causes or evidence of a design for despotism.

The rights of a people to declare their independence and alter their form of government exist in order to secure the rights to life, liberty, and the pursuit of happiness of the individuals who constitute the people. These rights therefore can be exercised only when the rights to life, liberty, and the pursuit of happiness are violated and endangered, that is, when necessary. Therefore, the American people did not declare independence at the first abuse or usurpation, but, on the contrary, "in every stage of these oppressions . . . petitioned for redress in the most humble terms." This humble posture should not have been misconstrued by the British as a lack of spirit, for it was accompanied by the actions of the representative bodies of the American people "opposing with manly firmness" the king's invasions of the rights of the people they represented. Indeed, the right of representation in the legislature may be "inestimable" to the people "and formidable to tyrants only" precisely because their representatives are supposed to oppose invasions of their rights with such manly firmness. Representatives represent the manly spirit as well as the desires of their constituents. This juncture of humble petitions with manly opposition nonetheless indicates a fundamental problem.

The first of the rights of individuals to be secured by governments and therefore by popular alterations and abolitions of governments is the right to life, yet such alterations require the people, like their representatives in the Declaration, to pledge their lives to each other, a pledge that some of them may have to make good. How can men give their lives to secure their right to life? While liberty is understood as a means to the preservation of life in order to justify taking the lives of others, in defense of one's own liberty, it must be considered more than such a means in order to justify risking one's own life in its defense. The defense of the right to life differs from the mere calculated defense of one's life—it is a spirited defense of a right, a claim that should be respected by others and vindicated by oneself.[27]

What if a people put their lives before their liberties or their rights, submitting to despotism or tyranny instead of opposing it with manly firmness? What if they do not do what is morally necessary but submit to a cruder kind of necessity? The Declaration, like the theory of Locke, seems to make the inalienable rights of individuals depend, for their practical security, as distinguished from their theoretical validity, in the first place on governments and ultimately on peoples, that is, on the manly firmness of peoples in defending their rights. This theory gives individuals their fundamental rights on the ground of their rationality or their moral sense.[28] But by making the security of those rights depend on resistance by the people it makes those rights depend practically on spirited self-defense, almost as if courage or the spirited will to vindicate one's rights were what entitled one to rights. The proper way for individuals' rights to be secured is for their own government or, failing that, for their own people to secure them. No other people or government or party has the right to secure the rights of those who have not consented to give them that right. Thus this theory puts a premium on spirited self-defense by a people of its own rights.

Some aspects of this complex position of spiritedness in the Declaration of Independence can be clarified by other public statements of the Continental Congress leading up to the Declaration. Most of these are documents of proto-foreign policy, addressing the King, the British people, the Canadians, the Irish, the Jamaicans, or the Indians. For example, even before it became necessary to abandon humble petitions for a final declaration, Congress was dismayed to find its "long forbearance rewarded with the imputation of cowardice."[29] They were proud that their dedication to peace had led them to postpone resort to arms as long as possible, but they feared that the result was doubt of their spirited willingness to fight for their rights when necessary. They had told the king that they thought themselves "required by indispensable obligations to Almighty God, to your Majesty, to our fellow subjects, and to ourselves, immediately to use all the means in our power not incompatible with our safety, for stopping the further effusion of blood," but the result seemed to be only that they were "vilified as wanting spirit."[30] Perhaps to avoid this impression among the British as well as to inspirit their fellow Americans, Congress emphasized that despite their dedication to the rights of life and property and the superficial appearance of a conflict over petty taxes, their love of liberty would lead Americans if necessary to risk and give their lives.

Congress stressed repeatedly that the danger was to liberty, reaching ultimately to its entire loss and replacement by slavery.[31] They assured the British that they had shown forbearance not "influenced by Fear or any other unworthy Motive," but because "the Lives of *Britons* are still dear to us." Yet Congress went only so far as to swear that "we would part with our Property, endanger our Lives, and sacrifice every thing but Liberty, to redeem you from ruin."[32] This assurance of loyalty was simultaneously a warning of resistance, of willingness to sacrifice loyalty to liberty. The breaking off of commercial intercourse with Britain was similarly presented as "the last peaceable admonition, that our attachment to no nation upon earth should supplant our attachment to liberty."[33]

Congress vividly represented Americans' love of liberty and abhorrence of slavery. They warned the king that the "apprehension of being degraded into a state of servitude" together with "the strongest love of liberty . . . excites emotions in our breasts . . . we cannot describe."[34] Above all, they proclaimed the superiority of liberty over life, of death over slavery. They repeatedly declared their determination "to live free, or not at all," "to dye Free-men rather than to live Slaves," "since even in Death we shall find that Freedom which in Life you forbid us to enjoy."[35]

The superiority of liberty over property was made even more clear. Congress admonished the British that the destruction of America's towns and the ravaging of its seacosts were "inconsiderable Objects, Things of no Moment to Men, whose bosoms glow with the Ardor of Liberty."[36] Addressing the Roman Catholics of Quebec, Congress appealed to their knowledge that "the transcendant nature of freedom elevates those, who unite in her cause, above all such low minded infirmities" as religious prejudice.[37] Such a love of liberty transcended both calculation of the odds and the satisfaction of desire.

Because the love of liberty transcended practical calculations, it could be of practical political and military value. Congress warned the British that the Americans as a people, not only "trained to Arms from their Infancy" but "animated by the Love of Liberty, will afford neither a cheap or easy Conquest." Conversely, if the British were willing to fight against the Americans "under the Banners of Tyranny" and "become the Instruments of Oppression," their arms would lose "their accustomed Vigour" without "the Spirit of Freedom, by which alone they are invincible."[38] The spirit of freedom is the spiritedness of a free people. In a practical sense it can be the spirit of freedom that makes and keeps a people free. In this spirit and in the name of Montesquieu, that "great advocate of freedom and humanity," Congress assured the Canadians that "the happiness of a people inevitably depends on their liberty, and their spirit to assert it."[39] The spirit of liberty is the spirited assertion of liberty. The spirit of liberty and not liberty alone secures political happiness.

The Americans found "nothing so dreadful as voluntary slavery."[40] Even worse than that lack of liberty which is involuntary or hereditary slavery is that lack of the spirit of liberty which allows those who enjoy liberty to submit to voluntary slavery. Thus it would be worse for the Americans, born free, to submit to tyranny than to have been born enslaved. Congress remarked:

> Had our creator been pleased to give us existence in a land of slavery, the sense of our condition might have been mitigated by ignorance and habit. But thanks be to his adoreable goodness, we were born the heirs of freedom.[41]

Similarly, when Congress explained to the Assembly of Jamaica that Americans refused "a submission, which spirits, unaccustomed to slavery, could not brook," they tacitly indicated that spirits accustomed to slavery could well brook such a submission.[42] The worst aspect of voluntary slavery seems to be the implication that those who lack the spirit of freedom and give up their freedom deserve the slavery they submit to. Congress concluded of the terms offered by Lord North that "to accept them would be to deserve them."[43] The spirit to assert one's liberty is therefore not merely a means to preserve liberty but part of what entitles one to liberty.

The obligation to defend one's liberty, which makes the failure to do so an act whereby one deserves to lose it, is an obligation not only to one's contemporaries but also to one's ancestors and posterity. Congress declared, "Honor, justice, and humanity forbid us tamely to surrender that freedom which we received from our gallant ancestors, and which our innocent posterity have a right to receive from us"[44] This obligation is in part one of gratitude for the gallantry or spirit of one's ancestors. Just as the Americans imitate "the unconquerable spirit" of their forefathers, the original settlers, so do they believe that the Canadians retain their "sense of honor" and have not "so degenerated as to possess neither the spirit, the gallantry, nor the courage of their ancestors" and "will not permit the infamy and disgrace of such pusillanimity to rest on your own heads, and the consequences of it on your children forever."[45] The spirit of liberty seems to be closely related to this sense of honor that recognizes the gratitude owed to the spirit of liberty of one's ancestors. This sense of honor aspires to perpetuate itself in the spirit of liberty of future heirs of freedom.[46] We can understand more clearly how the Declaration of Independence could culminate in a pledge of sacred honor.

The addresses of Congress to the various peoples of the British empire suggest a comparative political psychopathology, a survey of the alternatives to the spirit of liberty that entitles a people to be free. The Canadians seem the least blameworthy and the most promising, "educated under another form of government, [they] have artfully been kept from discovering the unspeakable worth" of freedom. They can be truly said to have been "conquered into liberty," if they now have "the spirit to assert it."[47] It is as if all they need to do is read the hundreds of copies of the letters from Congress translated into French explaining the rights they are entitled to in order to welcome the liberating American army. This is probably not the last time Americans were to misjudge the spirit of liberty of another people, either their willingness to embrace free government or their willingness to resist being conquered into liberty. In contrast, the maxims of freedom were known by the British, but "luxury and dissipation had diminished the wonted reverence for them," opening the way for corruption by a ministry with a deliberate plan to destroy the free constitution.[48] Although the Americans believed there was "yet much virtue, much justice, and much public spirit in the English nation," Britain had shown such "supineness" that there was "reason to suspect she has either ceased to be virtuous, or been extremely negligent."[49] In India, finally, "the effeminacy of the inhabitants promised an easy conquest" for the designs of the British ministry.[50] The Americans combined knowledge of the maxims of freedom with the spirit of freedom, being neither corrupted by luxury nor enervated by effeminacy. Neither ignorant spirit nor dispirited knowledge was sufficient to preserve liberty.[51]

Recognition of the importance of the spirit of liberty may mitigate the potential universalist doctrinairism implicit in the theory of the American founding. It is not enough to declare the rights of other peoples to entitle them in practice to liberty, let alone to practical assistance from other free peoples. They must manifest both knowledge of their rights and the spirit to assert them. (As the Canadian example shows, even this high standard can be applied on the basis of mistaken judgments.) In less spirited language, one must consider consent as well as rights. The proper means whereby individuals' rights are secured is the establishment of a government deriving its just powers from the consent of a people. Americans must consider not only the rights of all men everywhere, but whether particular peoples actually have consented to or have withdrawn their consent from their governments. A distinction must be made between those trying to defend their liberty from those ignorant of liberty or lacking the spirit to assert it.

Recognition of the importance of the spirit of liberty therefore helps to explain Alexander Hamilton's distinction between "justifiable and meritorious" assistance to a nation that "is in the act of liberating itself," such as French aid to the American

Revolution, and "a general invitation to insurrection and revolution," such as the French Revolution issued. The French treated "as enemies the people who, refusing or renoucing liberty and equality, are desirous of preserving their prince and privileged castes."[52] Henry Clay in the same spirit said he would not "disturb the repose of a detestable despotism," but he would aid an oppressed people who "will their freedom" and seek to establish or have established it.[53] The willingness to make such distinctions enables a free people to steer a course between the vain effort to conquer into liberty peoples unable or unwilling to exercise their liberty and the complacent assumption that all "those who are worthy of freedom, and will take care of it, have it."[54] The willingness to make such distinctions depends on giving weight to the spirit of liberty.

Recognition of the importance of the spirit of liberty may protect us from indulgence as well as from doctrinairism. If we cannot safely rely on the doctrine of liberty without the spirit to assert it, then we cannot afford the satisfaction of even every innocent or humane desire at the expense of spirited self-defense. If vindication of our rights is both the best means to preserve rights and a sign of our deserving to possess them, then we cannot regard it as necessarily a contribution to safety or justice to let others violate our rights with impunity. If our founding offers a model of the positive role of spiritedness, we may enjoy our liberty in the spirit of liberty.

Notes

1. Joseph Cropsey, *Political Philosophy and the Issues of Politics* (Chicago and London: University of Chicago Press, 1977), p.15.
2. Ibid., pp. 6–7.
3. *First Treatise*, sec. 1.
4. *Second Treatise*, secs. 17, 23.
5. Cf. Leo Strauss, *Natural Right and History*, (Chicago: University of Chicago Press, 1953), pp. 278–79 and n. 46.
6. On the connection between spiritedness and freedom, see Aristotle,

Politics VII.7; see also Harvey C. Mansfield, Jr., *The Spirit of Liberalism* (Cambridge, Mass.: Harvard University Press, 1978), p. 7.

7. *Second Treatise,* sec. 23.
8. *Second Treatise,* secs. 61, 63.
9. *First Treatise,* sec. 67; see also *Second Treatise,* sec. 4.
10. *Second Treatise,* sec. 196.
11. Ibid., sec. 239.
12. Epistle Dedicatory, *Some Thoughts Concerning Education,* in *The Educational Writing of John Locke,* ed. James Axtell (Cambridge, England: Cambridge University Press, 1968), pp. 112–13.
13. Ibid., secs. 103–10, 143, 116, 115, 126.
14. *First Treatise,* sec. 10; *Second Treatise,* secs. 34, 107, 111, 199, 230.
15. *Thoughts,* secs. 41, 73, 81; see also sec. 119.
16. Ibid., secs. 73, 148.
17. See *Thoughts,* secs. 76, 129; cf. Hobbes, *Leviathan,* chap. 11; Machiavelli, *Discourses* I:37, II pr., and chap. 9 of this volume, Michael Allen Gillespie, "Death and Desire: War and Bourgeoisification," pp. 172–73.
18. *Thoughts,* sec. 35; see also secs. 103, 119.
19. Cf. Hobbes, *Leviathan* 17, beginning: men "naturally love Liberty and Dominion over others."
20. *Thoughts,* secs. 31–39, 75, 106–08; *An Essay Concerning Human Understanding,* ed. Peter H. Nidditch (Oxford: Oxford University Press, 1975), II, xxi, 47, 52–53.
21. *Thoughts,* secs. 56–58, 61, 185, 200.
22. Contrast Locke, *Two Tracts on Government,* ed. Philip Abrams (Cambridge, England: Cambridge University Press, 1967), pp. 120, 140.
23. *Thoughts,* secs. 45–47; see also sec. 102.
24. Ibid., secs. 46, 50, 51. Locke used spirit or spirits in both a physiological sense, as in "an habitual Motion of the Animal Spirits," which appears in connection with thoughts, digestion, excretion, and courage, and in a metaphysical sense, as in "other *Spirits,* besides God, and our own Souls," meaning "*immaterial Beings.*" Here the usage is closer to the former sense, if we may assume a clear disjunction between those two senses (*Thoughts,* secs. 25, 115, 136–38, 190–192).
25. See Cropsey's remarks on "the spirited desire of man for self-dependence," which carries man up to "the noble simulation of independence by the dependent," *Political Philosophy,* p. 226.

26. On the problem of necessity and choice in the Declaration, see Mansfield, *The Spirit of Liberalism*, pp. 72–88.

27. In a remarkable passage in his notes on the debate in Congress on March 4, 1776, leading up to independence, John Adams presented resentment and punishment of injury as both a means to preservation and a duty: "Resentment is a passion implanted by nature for the preservation of the individual. Injury is the object which excites it. . . . A man may have the faculty of concealing his resentment, or suppressing it, but he must and ought to feel it; nay, he ought to indulge it, to cultivate it; it is a duty. His person, his property, his liberty, his reputation, are not safe without it. He ought, for his own security and honor, and for the public good, to punish those who injure him, unless they repent, and then he should forgive, having satisfaction and compensation. Revenge is unlawful. It is the same with communities; they ought to resent and to punish" (Worthington Chauncey Ford, Ed., *Journals of the Continental Congress*, vol. 6 [Washington: Government Printing Office, 1906], p. 1074). Compare Edmund Burke to Claude-François de Rivarol, June 1, 1791: "That fury which arises in the minds of men on being stripped of their goods, and turned out of their houses by acts of power, and our sympathy with them under Such wrongs, are feelings implanted in us by our creator to be (under the direction of his laws) the means of our preservation. . . . They arise out of instinctive principles of self defence and are executive powers under the legislation of nature, enforcing its first law" (*Selected Letters of Edumnd Burke*, ed. Harvey C. Mansfield, Jr. [Chicago: University of Chicago Press, 1984], p. 291.

28. Jefferson seemed to base rights not on rationality but on the moral sense: see the discussion of blacks in *Notes on the State of Virginia*, chap. 14.

29. "An Address to the People of Ireland," July 28, 1775, in *A Decent Respect to the Opinions of Mankind: Congressional State Papers 1774–1776* (Washington: Library of Congress, 1975), p. 113.

30. Ibid., p. 115; "The Olive Branch Petition," July 8, 1775, p. 129; also "Report on Lord North's Conciliatory Proposal," July 3, 1775, p. 129; also "Report on Lord North's Conciliatory Proposal," July 3, 1775, p. 122.

31. Ibid., "To the People of Great-Britain," October 21, 1774, pp. 23, 25, 27, 29; "The Bill of Rights and List of Grievances," October 1774, p. 55; "Petition to the King," October 25, 1774, p. 77; "To

the Oppressed Inhabitants of Canada," May 29, 1775, p. 85; "Declaration of the Causes and Necessity of Taking Up Arms," July 6, 1775, pp. 91, 96; "To the Inhabitants of Great Britain," July 8, 1775, p. 102.

32. Ibid., "To the Inhabitants of Great Britain," pp. 105, 108.

33. Ibid., "Declaration of the Causes and Necessity of Taking Up Arms," p. 93.

34. Ibid., "Petition to the King," p. 77.

35. Ibid., "To the Oppressed Inhabitants of Canada," p. 86; "Declaration of the Causes and Necessity of Taking Up Arms," p. 96; "To the Inhabitants of Great Britain," p. 107.

36. Ibid., "To the Inhabitants of Great Britain," p. 104.

37. Ibid., "A Letter to the Inhabitants of the Province of Quebec," October 26, 1774, p. 67. A few days earlier, however, in addressing the people of Great Britain, Congress had referred to the Roman Catholicism of Quebec as "a religion fraught with sanguinary and impious tenets" that "has deluged your island in blood, and dispersed impiety, bigotry, persecution, murder and rebellion through every part of the world" ("To the People of Great-Britain," pp. 24, 29).

38. Ibid., "To the Inhabitants of Great Britain," pp. 104, 107.

39. Ibid., "A Letter to the Inhabitants of the Province of Quebec," p. 67.

40. Ibid., "Declaration of the Causes and Necessity of Taking Up Arms," p. 95.

41. Ibid., "Petition to the King," p. 77.

42. Ibid., "Address to the Assembly of Jamaica," July 25, 1775, p. 136.

43. Ibid., "Declaration of the Causes and Necessity of Taking Up Arms," p. 94. Cf. Cropsey's argument that "We will prove his right to rule us if we do not prevent him from exercising it" (*Political Philosophy*, p. 183).

44. *A Decent Respect to the Opinions of Mankind*, "Declaration of the Causes and Necessity of Taking Up Arms," p. 95; see also "To the Inhabitants of Great Britain," pp. 103–04; "To the People of Ireland," p. 116.

45. Ibid., 'To the Oppressed Inhabitants of Canada," p. 86; "Declaration of the Causes and Necessity of Taking Up Arms," p. 91.

46. Cf. Cropsey's remarks on the connection between rights and honor, *Political Philosophy*, pp. 187–88.

47. *A Decent Respect to the Opinions of Mankind*, "A Letter to the In-

habitants of the Province of Quebec," pp. 61, 67. Locke too provides for the possibility of being conquered into liberty. Although
he generally allows conquered peoples the right to revolt when it
is "worth the Trouble and Cost," they do not have the right to
revolt to assume independence if their conquerors either put them
under a frame of government they freely consent to or at least allow
them or their representatives to give free consent to laws and taxes
(*Second Treatise*, secs. 176, 192). Thus the Canadians would have
been truly "conquered into liberty" and the Americans would not
have had the need or right to revolt if both had been conceded the
benefits of the British constitution under which the people have,
not the whole legislative power as in a democracy, but "a share—
together with the King and Lords—in their own government, by
their representatives . . . a bulwark surrounding and defending their
property . . . so that no portions of it can legally be taken from them,
but with their own full and free consent" ("A Letter to the Inhabitants of the Province of Quebec," p. 62).

48. *A Decent Respect to the Opinions of Mankind*, "Address to the As-
    sembly of Jamaica," p. 135.
49. Ibid., "To the People of Great Britain," pp. 23, 30.
50. Ibid., "Address to the Assembly of Jamaica," p. 135.
51. Cf. Aristotle, *Politics* VII.7, and chapter 3 of this volume, Ann
    Charney, "Spiritedness and Piety in Aristotle," pp. 79–80.
52. *Pacificus*, no. 2, *The Works of Alexander Hamilton*, ed. Henry Cabot
    Lodge (New York, 1904), vol. 4, pp. 451, 453.
53. "Emancipation of the South American States," *The Works of Henry
    Clay*, ed. Calvin Colton (New York, 1904), vol. 6, p. 142.
54. Rep. Abraham W. Venable, *The Congressional Globe*, vol. 22, pt.
    2, 32d Cong., 2d sess., January 3, 1853, p. 191.

MICHAEL
GILLESPIE

IX

Death and Desire: War and Bourgeoisification in the Thought of Hegel

Many thinkers of varying political stripes have argued that the growing bourgeoisification of modern life represents a real and ominous threat to man's humanity. Attempts to counteract this tendency, however, have often ended in disaster. In this chapter I argue that bourgeoisification is the result of a peculiarly modern understanding of death which legitimates the pursuit of peace and pleasure while undermining the spirited pursuit of martial glory characteristic of the ancient world. In the bulk of the chapter I examine Hegel's attempt to remedy this tendency by showing how these ancient and modern alternatives can be reconciled on the basis of a new understanding of death. Finally, I try to assess Hegel's argument and determine its relevance for us today.

Death and the Structure of Human Life

Man's understanding of death has always played a crucial role in determining the structure of human life. This is hardly surprising, since the character or meaning of a thing is determined on one hand by what it is in itself and on the other by what it is not. The character of a thing is thus a function of its form or limits. The character of human life, however, is not easily determined, since man is not merely in himself but also for himself. Man's determinate being is thus in part a reflection of his self-understanding, which is primarily an understanidng of his own limits. This is especially true of death. Death is the limit of human life but its meaning remains a question, since man can have no experience or positive knowledge of it. Death is always out-standing and unknown. How we stand toward death, however, is decisive for our stance toward life. Our understanding of death thus determines in many respects how we lead our lives and how we believe life ought to be led.

The Greeks recognized death as essential to human life and understood man in contrast to the immortal gods and eternal nature as a mortal being. In their view man's ethical and political obligations arise out of the recognition and acceptance of mor-tality. To be a man is to "know thyself" and to do "everything in measure," that is, to know one is not a god and to act according to the human measure as a mortal being. The Greek understand-ing of death establishes an injunction against both hubris and cowardice that delimits political life. To be human one must face death with a spirited courage that accepts its inevitability. One thus neither flees from death nor attempts to overcome it. This recognition of death as the essential element of man's human being directs one instead to the polis that is the true source of human immortality, that is, of immortal fame. Individual im-mortality, as the Greeks saw it, is beyond man, and species immortality is shared with the animals. What is distinctively human is the immortality of recollection engendered by glorious deeds. This immortality, however, is thus only granted to those whose self-sacrifice and courageous acceptance of death in battle serve to preserve the polis. The Christian conception of death also establishes guidelines for morality and politics. For Chris-tianity death does not distinguish man from gods but provides the link between man and God. It represents not the end of human life and happiness but the beginning of immortality and divine beatitude. The recognition of the inevitability of death, then, does not direct man to a courageous or spirited life in support of the polis but a saintly and otherworldly emulation of the divine.

For modernity, death is not essential to human life but is

accidental. It is neither an ineluctable end that must be coura-
geously confronted nor the gateway to salvation; it is extrinsic
and alien to life and ought to be resisted and overcome. This
modern understanding of death rests upon a redefinition of the
human being as subjectivity. Man's being does not depend upon
nature or the divine but only upon itself. Unlike other natural
things, man is self-conscious and autonomous, an end in himself.
His naturalness is something that must be overcome, for to be
human is to be free from nature and natural necessity. The goal
of both modern natural science and modern political science is
the liberation of man from the limitations nature imposes upon
him, that is, from death and suffering. Man as a self-conscious
subject thus turns to a technological conquest and transformation of the natural world to secure human preservation and
prosperity.

This impulse lies at the heart of modern liberalism and
threatens to reduce man to homo economicus. This has a decisive
effect upon the worth of human capacities and activities. Courage
and spiritedness, for example, become less important. Success
in liberal societies, Tocqueville points out, depends upon regular
and unimpassioned habits, such as those of the businessman. The
spirited virtues admired in the ancient world thus come to be
regarded as anti-social and brutish.

Liberalism has often been criticized for its pursuit of pleasure and preservation. Rousseau pointed out that the development
of modern science and technology undermined virtue and human
freedom. Nietzsche even more pessimistically saw the consequences of liberalism in the "last man" for whom everything
has become a mere object of gratification. For Heidegger and
existentialism, liberalism ends with the triumph of the "they"
who are entangled in the inauthentic world of natural and tech-
nical instrumentalities. These thinkers call for a rejection of the
bourgeois world in favor of a more virile and virtuous life.

Resistance to bourgeoisification, however, has been inef-
fective. Despite revolutionary and totalitarian interludes, the hegemony of economic life has expanded and solidified. Those
dissatisfied with this development have been driven to seek ever

more radical solutions. While Rousseau thought man might be "forced to be free," Nietzsche saw the necessity of an overman for whom "everything is permitted," and Heidegger asserted that man must cast himself into the abyss of nihilism and death to retrieve his humanity.

The failure of modernity to accept death as essential to human life propels man into a new confrontation with death. However, this confrontation does not lead man back to political life but casts him instead into a radical individualism. Death is understood not as a common human fate but as man's "ownmost possibility" that radically severs him from his fellows. Ironically, this is nowhere so evident as in the collectivist efforts of both the left and the right in this century. Unable to persuade man to abandon economic self-interest, collectivists have used brutal force, destroying the human basis for community and opening the way for the rule of men who lust for the absolute power of death. Modernity's initial premise that death is something to be overcome consequently makes power the crux of human life. The banality of homo economicus produces homo brutalitas. Any resolution to this dilemma thus requires an understanding of human existence that accepts death as necessary but does not plunge man into a nihilistic pursuit of unlimited power. It is such an understanding that Hegel claims to present.

Death and Desire: Hegel's Notion of Master and Slave

Hegel defines man's humanity as self-conscious in the famous chapter on "Self-consciousness" in the *Phenomenology*. Originally man is merely conscious of the world and has no awareness of himself as a distinct entity. He does not distinguish himself from the object he perceives and in a sense is that object. With the advent of self-consciousness, man recognizes himself as an autonomous being. This moment of transcendence and liberation, however, is also a moment of separation and alienation, for as self-consciousness man is severed from the world that seemed to constitute his being. He is alienated from himself and his autonomy and self-sufficiency are challenged by the otherness of this alien object. In response, man attempts to overcome and subordinate the other in order to reconstitute the original unity. This attempt to overcome alienation is the essence of desire.

Desire for Hegel is not an animalistic drive for satisfaction arising from a natural need. Rather, it is the consequence of a split in consciousness between self and world. Its satisfaction depends not on the reestablishment of a natural physical balance but on the reconciliation of the underlying split or alienation. In its most rudimentary form desire attempts to overcome this split in two basic ways, by the physical consumption of animate nature and the appropriation of inanimate nature as property. Neither of these forms of desire, however, can satisfy self-consciousness. Both are negations of otherness that subordinate the external object to the self. However, insofar as these objects are incorporated within or infused by the self, they cease to be objects for self-consciousness, and self-consciousness itself is thereby thrown back into alienation. Desire enlarges the sphere of the self but it does not confirm man's notion of himself as an autonomous being. The end of self-consciousness is not the sensuous object but unity with itself, that is, self-certainty.[1] Self-consciousness attains self-certainty only through the subordination of another self-consciousness, of an object that is also a subject capable of recognizing and affirming the other's independence. Satisfaction is achieved only if desire becomes spiritedness and turns upon itself in a life and death struggle for domination.

In his early thought Hegel considered the possibility that the distinction of self and other could be overcome through love but later recognized that love could not achieve such a reconciliation.[2] A fundamental reconciliation, in his view, must encompass the most antagonistic elements. Love depends not upon mutual antagonism but upon mutual attraction. Thus, while a mutuality of desire is necessary for self-consciousness to attain self-certainty and reconciliation with itself, this desire takes the form of a spirited assertiveness.[3]

This spirited struggle orginates as a dispute over property.

Property is a product of desire: it is the extension of the will and thus of the self into objects. A thing is mine because in a literal sense it is *me*. The appropriation of property by the individual, however, imposes a barrier to the universal appropriation of property by others and thus to each individual's autonomy and self-certainty. What man desires is, from his point of view, his own externalized or alienated self.[4] To be excluded from what is desired is therefore to be excluded from one's own being. The consequence of this discovery of another self in what one takes to be one's own being is a struggle to demonstrate the universality of one's own being against this intruder.[5]

This war of all against all, which Hobbes in Hegel's view correctly recognized as the true state of nature, is not a mere physical struggle but one to determine whose rights shall prevail.[6] The right to own property derives from self-consciousness, since only those beings who are self-conscious and therefore free can put their will into objects and make them their own. The struggle for recognition is thus a struggle to determine who can rightfully claim the world as his own, that is, whose will in fact infuses the object.[7] To be self-conscious is to be in and for oneself, to be the cause of one's own action and therefore not subject to the causality that characterizes natural phenomena. Nature, however, appears for man as life and desire. Hence, freedom from nature means freedom from life and thus is a choice for death as the willingness to face death to preserve one's freedom. Self-consciousness is the source of the courage to choose a free death rather than a life of bondage. The courageous have rights not because they conquer but because their courage is a manifestation of their will to freedom. The right to property, even the right to one's own body, depends upon independence from all property, including the property one has in one's own body. Without this, independence becomes a slave to property. Only those are free who, in Kantian terms, are unwilling to be treated as means and insist to the death upon being treated as ends in themselves.[8]

The war of all against all consequently determines who is

free, who has rights, and who is a human being. This is not, however, merely a historical struggle among men.[9] It is also and perhaps primarily a psychological struggle within each man.[10] In the absence of conflict all men are dominated by desire and extend themselves in all directions through consumption and the accumulation of property. However, desire confronts desire and the ensuing conflict produces a transformation not just in the relationship between men but in the soul of each. The external conflict activates the latent conflict in the soul between a desire for pleasure and preservation and a desire for freedom.[11] Victory over the external other depends on the conquest of the internal other, that is, on the conquest of nature as it manifests itself in one's own soul. Only if desire can be subordinated to freedom can man subordinate others to his will. Man's struggle for mastery over others is hence the source of his mastery over himself, thus the beginning of his spiritual vocation.[12]

This struggle aims at a demonstration of independence and totality. It is joined not to kill or enslave others but to demonstrate one's own freedom and humanity by facing death.[13] In a sense, it is an attempt at suicide as a proof of freedom.[14] At first glance it would seem that all truly free men must be dead. Indeed, Hegel points to this conclusion in the *Phenomenology* to show the dialectical insufficiency of this primitive mode of self-consciousness. In his earlier and later work, however, he recognizes that the risk of death at the hands of another is sufficient to demonstrate one's freedom from nature.[15]

The result of this life and death struggle is the differentiation of human beings into masters and slaves. The master proves his freedom and independence through his willingness to die while the slave surrenders because he desires something other than freedom. The spirited justly come to rule in this way over those dominated by desire. The slave is really a slave not to his master but to life, and he says by his act that he is not free.[16] Without the consciousness of freedom, however, he sinks to the level of a thing and can legitimately be held as property.[17] The natural inequality that comes to light in this struggle is the result not of physical disparities or the vagaries of fortune but of an internal imbalance in the soul of the slave. Society mirrors the psyche.[18]

The master's triumph, however, does not ultimately lift him above natural desire, and the slave's desire for preservation and pleasure does not ultimately deprive him of his humanity. In Hegel's view both elements are incomplete and are mutually necessary for a truly human life. Their reconciliation arises from the intrinsic instability of the master–slave relationship itself. The master seeks and wins recognition through the life and death struggle but subsequently falls back into a life devoted to consumption and enjoyment. His enjoyment, however, is no longer the result of his subordination of an alien object but of his perfect communion with a world that is already subordinate to or infused by his will. This communion is made possible by the slave, who stands between the master and the alien world, transforming it through work into a form appropriate for immediate consumption. The master's life is thus pure and effortless pleasure while the slave's is continual and unrelenting drudgery.

The bliss of the master and the degradation of the slave, however, are only momentary and apparent: the master's victory proves to be the source of his downfall and the slave's defeat the source of his ultimate triumph. The master is corrupted by his own independence. The slave satisfies him, thereby removing all opposition. The master's internal mastery of his desires, however, was made possible by the presence of an antagonist and in the absence of such an opponent he is unable to restrain his desire. His life degenerates into pure hedonism; hegemony produces decadence.

The slave who sought to escape death, by contrast, is continually confronted by it in the shape of his master. Despite himself he is driven into self-consciousness and humanity. The slave's autonomy, though, is not attained through a spirited struggle with others but through his transformation of the natural world by work. The natural world presents an obstacle for consciousness. Man tries to subdue it through consumption, the appropriation of property, and the subjugation of others, but these prove insufficient. The work of the slave, according to Hegel, is a more fundamental means of overcoming the disjunction of man and nature. Work does not consume or claim the world but recreates it in man's own image for his use. Work thus succeeds where desire and spiritedness failed. Man's humanity comes to express itself in work, and man himself becomes homo economicus. The humanity of homo economicus, however, is dependent upon the fear of the master, that is, the fear of death.[19] Indeed, the slave can only transcend and transform nature because of the fear of death that the master engenders. Without this fear, homo economicus falls below the level of humanity.

The master-slave relationship is thus the basic form of political life. The family is older than the state, but it depends upon love and property while the state embodies general freedom or spirit. General freedom, however, can only be attained by a master who subordinates both his own desires and those of the men and women he conquers to his own indomitable will to freedom. Without such a master, a people is not a state but a mass or agglomeration of individuals who are moved not by a free and rational purpose but by the caprice of their natural passions.[20]

The actual beginning of the state thus lies in the struggle to determine who is free and has the right to property both in land and in the bodies of other human beings. The basis of rule by the spirited or courageous is not force or coercion but the demonstration of their freedom.[21] While the state consequently begins in despotism, this despotism represents the basic rational element that brings the anarchy of the passions to an end.[22] The state arises through force but it is a force in the service of freedom and hence of right. The man who exercises this force is the embodiment of right. He is a hero, and his exercise of force is an example of "the right of heroes."[23]

The master-slave relationship is essential only at the beginning of a regime and is retained thereafter only as a superseded moment in the structure of authority.[24] This does not mean, however, that homo economicus is essential to all succeeding regimes.[25] Politics, in Hegel's view, is not economics but rather the subordination of nature to freedom or of desire to spiritedness and reason in the form of law. Homo economicus is capable of exercising political power only if he can embody the master's will to freedom and transcend his own individual desires. Hegel doubts, however, that homo economicus can ever free himself from his desires and truly rule. Thus, even in the rational state, the leaders in the economic sphere are dependent upon the military and the bureaucracy to maintain political life. The modern world may well be dominated by desire but in Hegel's view this desire and its embodiment in economic life are made possible and tempered by spiritedness under the hegemony of wisdom.

War and Economic Life in the Modern State

Desire manifests itself in the modern world as the unlimited pursuit of property in a highly differentiated economic system by individuals organized into corporate bodies. Hegel calls this system bourgeois or civil society. While desire in this context is divorced from the state, it is not antithetical to freedom but harmonious with it. This harmony, however, cannot become an identity since desire remains rooted in natural need. In fact bourgeois society leads to an enormous expansion of needs and of the capacity to satisfy them through an ever-increasing expansion of the market and division of labor. This produces problems: the ease of obtaining satisfaction gives rise to a narrow hedonism unconcerned with virtue or free institutions and the division of labor produces trenchant class distinctions between a wealthy few and a pauperized rabble. This combination of hedonism and misery dissolves social unity and promotes revolution. This is exacerbated by the fact that liberal theorists not only fail to recognize the necessity of supervening state institutions to secure general freedom but also argue that the state is merely a tool for adjudicating disputes. Thus, bourgeois society undermines virtue, disrupts communal life, and consistently attacks the only institution that can preserve human freedom.

The rationality and freedom of the modern state can only be maintained, in Hegel's view, by restraining and limiting bourgeois society in the interest of the state as a whole. This is achieved by a liberally educated bureaucracy headed by an impartial monarch and council of advisors. The state apparatus represents the good of the whole in contradistinction to the good of the parts and uses its power to ameliorate the inordinate and socially undesirable disparities of wealth produced by the unfettered operation of the economy.

The capacity for such an impartial, administrative control of economic life is limited by the representative character of the legislative branch. Representative institutions insure that substantive economic interests are taken into account but, if they are too powerful, they can undermine the government's ability to transcend particularity in the interest of the general good. Consequently, Hegel thought that one house of the legislature should reflect corporate interests and that the other should rise above them. This is achieved by a hereditary upper house composed of large landholders who do not need to participate in economic life and are restrained from doing so by public opinion and their own notions of honor. However, they too represent a particular interest—landed property—although it has less immediate interest than the interests of the members of the lower house, who are drawn directly from corporations. Even the independent executive branch has great difficulty resisting economic forces, largely because it is generally concerned with the regulation of property in an adjudicative and redistributive capacity. The general freedom that this rational administration is supposed to maintain is thus in constant danger of degenerating into the aggregate interest of individual citizens and corporations.

The inability of reason alone to restrain and direct desire underlies the degeneration of the state into a tool of bourgeois or civil society. The modern state resembles the individual in the state of nature, who lacks the inner resolve to conquer his desire. Like this man, it must engage in a spirited, life and death struggle that suppresses desire and demonstrates the manifest reality of a general freedom.[26] Only in this way can the state transcend the particular economic interests of bourgeois society. War is thus intrinsic to the rational state and is the only viable restraint upon bourgeoisification and political degeneration.

War reveals the hard but necessary truth that all possessions, including one's own body and life, are transitory. This truth is obscured in modernity by the success of the liberal state in securing peace and opening up a realm for the proliferation of economic life. In the state of nature everyone feared death. Within the master-slave relationship the slave saw death before him in the shape of his master. The reconciliation of master and slave that Hegel saw as the result of historical development gradually concealed death. This leads to the loss of human freedom and a servitude to natural desire. The recurrence of war teaches man that the satisfaction of desire depends upon the state. Man's rights are not given; they depend upon the freedom and autonomy of the state. The threat of death thus diverts man from the pursuit of gain to the pursuit of freedom. According to Hegel, freedom is present in peacetime only in the external form of the state. In wartime the state shows itself as spirit or freedom when it exercises its power over the life, property, and particularity of the individual. War, then, preserves the health of the state; "just as the blowing of the wind preserves the sea from the foulness which would be the result of a long calm."[27]

Hegel sees a continual degeneration of freedom within the modern state brought about by the predominance of particularistic self-interest and believes that this degeneration can be restrained and freedom maintained only by a periodic return to the state of nature and that means to the state of war. This solution has much in common with the Jeffersonian idea of a periodic, revolutionary dissolution and reconstitution of the state to maintain the vitality of liberal institutions. Hegel, however, argues war better secures this end. Revolution throws men back into the state of nature and forces them to confront death as individuals, undermining all previous progress. War casts men as a group back into the state of nature and makes clear to them that they are always in a state of nature vis-à-vis other states and thus always in need of discipline and resolve. The experience of this truth, in Hegel's view, provides the rational elements in the state with the spirited fortitude necessary to maintain free institutions.

Hegel was suspicious of a revolutionary solution to the problem of bourgeois society because of the danger of fanaticism such as that of the Terror of the French Revolution. The chief danger to modern man, in his view, lies in the predominance of bourgeois society over the state. A less likely but more terrifying danger awaits man in the fanaticism of freedom that uses the state to crush bourgeois society in the attempt to transform human nature itself. Thus, while Hegel was anxious to prevent the degeneration of man into homo economicus, he was unwilling to risk a path that might lead to homo brutalitas. To avoid both hedonism and fanaticism, he turned to war.

The state, for Hegel, is the embodiment of freedom and reason in the world. A revolution against the state is legitimate only if it produces a more rational and freer state. The modern state, however, establishes the rational framework for the coexistence and reconciliation of human freedom and natural desire. Revolution thus can only strengthen the darker passions that positive law and public opinion restrain. By contrast, war strengthens the rationality of the state by evoking the latent general will and community spirit of the citizenry. In war, man recognizes the state as the source of rights and is lifted above self-interest and desire. War thus strengthens the attachment of individual citizens to the state. The danger is that a protracted war can brutalize society as a whole. Although securing the independence of the state is the highest duty of every citizen, it is better for the citizenry as a whole that the actual defense of the state be left to a professional army.[28] This army forms a distinct class that is characterized by courage and aims at the preservation of the state. The members of this class do not desire personal autonomy or recognition and thus are different from those who risked death to secure their freedom in the state of nature. They may be motivated by purely personal ends but their inner motives are irrelevant. Once in the ranks they are constrained by a notion of honor that compels them to face death whenever their courage is questioned.[29] It is likely that they will be drawn from those who are naturally courageous, but this is not necessary as it is their collective courage that is decisive and that is secured by the rational organization of the army and the state.

What is necessary from the army is a firm spiritual attachment to the state.[30] Contrary to what one might expect, technological advances in warfare, such as the gun, have increased the predominance of the spiritual element. This development, however, merely reflects the historical transformation of man and society that has produced individual freedom but also has integrated the individual in the state. Modern man thus goes to war not to conquer other individuals but to secure the freedom of his own state. He is spirited, but his spiritedness arises from his rational commitment to the state.

Although the ordinary defense of the state should be left to a professional army, all men, according to Hegel, must come to the defense of the state if necessary. To bring all citizens under arms, however, is extremely dangerous, as it is likely that what was a defensive war will thereby become a war of aggression. This is in part because the people en masse are more easily swayed by their passions than monarchs or cabinet ministers. A more important reason for this turn toward aggression is that people discover in war that war itself can serve as a means of acquiring property.[31] Thus, while defensive or retributive wars fought by professional armies can strengthen the state, wars that require universal conscription are likely to turn the state from the pursuit of autonomy to the pursuit of property. Although the absence of any war leads to the hedonism, misery, and class conflict of bourgeois society, too much war produces an aggressive and rapacious state dedicated to the accumulation of property. Without enough war, man is reduced to homo economicus; too much war turns him into a monstrous combination of homo economicus and homo brutalitas.

Fortunately, wars in Hegel's view, do not often reach this extreme. Most states aim at securing the recognition of their sovereignty or autonomy and are thus careful to retain the possibility of peace. They tacitly agree "that war not be waged against domestic institutions, against the peace of the family and private life, or against persons in their private capacity."[32] Wars become more humane due to the decreasing importance of the personal passions of the combatants and their respect for their adversary's rational attachment to his state.[33] That war becomes more humane, however, is no indication that it can be abolished.

Wars arise when a state feels that its sovereignty has been insulted, that is, when it feels it has not been recognized and treated as an autonomous being. In war the state demands that insults be avenged and its sovereignty acknowledged. What constitutes an insult, however, is a subjective judgment made by the state itself. The complexity of political relationships produces many incidents that can be construed as slights, but whether they are so construed depends upon the predisposition of the state to interpret them as such.[34] This predisposition in turn depends upon the internal strength and unity of the state.

The likelihood that a state will go to war, according to Hegel, is thus directly proportional to the weakness of state institutions. This weakness is not the consequence of poor leadership or organization but of the prolongation of peace. Peace leads to the predominance of the particularistic interests that characterize bourgeois society and undermine the general will of the state.[35] As a result, the sovereignty of the state over its own citizens is brought into doubt. This makes every injury that much more dangerous to stability. Every act that is injurious to the state is thus likely to be construed as an insult in part because of the real, increased danger to the state but also because the state can use a war to secure peace and stability at home.[36] Hegel thus thought that he had located a structural mechanism intrinsic to the state governing the relations of war and peace among nations. Wars thus occur not as the result of a fortuitous conjunction of circumstances but "when the necessity of the cases requires."[37]

Hegel also disagreed with the idea that success in war is the result of either chance or coercion. The strength of a state and the likelihood of its success in war depend rather upon its capacity to subordinate desire to freedom and autonomy. The state that is freer and more rational will thus be stronger because it more successfully unites individual self-interest and the general good. Every war in this sense is a test of the relative freedom and rationality of the states involved. Thus, the course of historical development, which seems to be a long series of bloody wars and revolutions in which mere force rules, is in fact the development of freedom and reason. In war both states claim to be right. Their notion of right, however, is only a reflection of their constitutions and the conception of justice upon which these constitutions rest. War decides which of these conceptions of justice better secures freedom and thus is more rational. War, then, decides which system of rights must give way and which shall prevail.[38] "World-history is the world-judge" not because might makes right but because right makes might, because the state that is more autonomous and rational is stronger than its less advanced antagonists.[39]

If victory is an indication of progress and rationality, defeat is a sure sign of decadence and the need for reform.[40] The sovereignty of a state, in Hegel's view, depends upon the recognition of its autonomy by other states and by its own citizens. The minimum requirement for such recognition is the capacity of the state to defend itself. The failure of a state to do so, however, is not the result of a lack of courage on the part of its soldiers but of a lack of effective institutions to organize this courage.[41] This institutional failure is only a reflection of the antiquated and historically irrational character of the state's constitution. Although defeat in the first instance is a reflection of internal political weakness, this weakness is only a reflection of a deeper spiritual weakness.

In this way philosophy becomes necessary to provide a new ground of unity for political life. Hegel argued that philosophy arises when the world with which we are familiar has become divided and self-contradictory.[42] Such division under-

mines the state, which becomes unable to restrain economic life
or defend itself. It is confronted with both internal dissolution
and external dismemberment. The state suffers the same fate as
the man in the state of nature who chose self-preservation over
freedom: it becomes enslaved.

Defeat, however, may be more profitable than victory.
Victory demonstrates the strength of a state's institutions but
does not improve them. It leaves the state with no substantive
task and thus with a life like that of the victorious master dedicated to pure enjoyment. The consequence is hedonism and
political degeneration. Defeat opens up the possibility of greater
rationality and freedom. The value of defeat, however, depends
upon the capacity of thought to respond to the need of philosophy
and articulate a new and more rational basis for political life.

The success of the modern state in restraining bourgeoisification and securing its autonomy thus ultimately depends upon
philosophy. This involves a determination of the rational basis
of the state and the articulation of the institutions necessary to
secure freedom and rationality. Fundamental to such a philosophy is a new and more profound understanding of the limits
of human life and thus of death. This understanding lies at the
core of Hegel's thought and informs his conception of political
life and political institutions.

A Brave New World?

Few modern thinkers have evinced as strong and enduring an
admiration for the ancient world as Hegel.[43] He recognized,
however, that a rebirth of ancient political life and the magnif-
icent individuality it had fostered was impossible because of the
development of bourgeois society. The bourgeois world, however, was not simply despicable, for however poorly it compared
to the "beautiful ethical life" of the Greeks, it embodied a greater
rationality and freedom than the ancients had ever known. Like
Rousseau before him and Nietzsche after him, Hegel hoped to
restrain the excessive bourgeoisification of modern life by a re-

vival of something like the spiritedness and virtue of antiquity. Unlike them he believed that these would naturally be brought out in the modern world by war.

This understanding of war and its role in restraining bourgeois life rests upon a new understanding of death that hearkens back to antiquity but does not abandon the goals of modernity. Unlike most moderns, Hegel regards death not as accidental or irrational but as intrinsic to the freedom that constitutes the human essence. Man is human insofar as he values freedom above life and desire. The freedom of the state as well rests upon a transcendence of desire, as it appears in bourgeois life, and thus upon the acceptance of death and war as necessary components of life. While death and war are essential to human life, however, they are not its end. Indeed, they are predominant only at the most primitive level of man's being and are necessary but not sufficient to his humanity. Here Hegel parts company with the ancients, pointing to the necessity of exercising one's freedom to transform the world through thought and work.

Although he argued that war is necessary, Hegel was not a warmonger, as some have contended.[44] War may be necessary but it is not good in itself and should not be pursued for its own sake. Hegel does not seek its abolition, however, because it restrains the universal greed that would result from "perpetual peace." This tacit acceptance of war also rests on his belief that wars will become increasingly humane as ideological differences wane and all states come to recognize human freedom as the sole legitimate end of political life.[45]

For all its profundity Hegel's view of the role of war in restraining bourgeois life is wrong in several respects, especially when measured against the melancholy history of the post-Hegelian world. First, he underestimated the strength and intractability of desire and thus failed to appreciate the strength of bourgeoisification and the danger of tyranny. Second, he believed that all ideological struggle had come to an end and thus did not recognize the necessity of precautions to prevent the administrative mechanisms of the rational state from being turned to the service of irrational ends. Finally, he did not foresee the transformation of modern wars, which he believed would reinforce rational administrative restraint of bourgeois society, from wars of maneuver fought by small professional armies into orgies of destruction engulfing populations. In short, Hegel was overly optimistic about the triumph of reason and thus did not grasp the irrationality intrinsic to human life.[46]

In this respect Hegel seems closer to the Enlightenment than to thinkers such as Nietzsche, Freud, and Heidegger with whom he has often been compared. The existentialist interpretation of Hegel in particular has tried to show that he had a profound understanding of the power of the irrational. Supporters of the view argue, for example, that the only difference between Hegel and Nietzsche is that Hegel found a way out of nihilism while Nietzsche discovered only the nihilistic joy of continual self-overcoming in the chaotic exercise of the will to power.[47] That Hegel grasped the authentic irrationality of human life or found a real solution to it, however, is doubtful. The logical ground of his solution is obscure to say the least.[48] Even disregarding these logical difficulties, the authenticity of the irrationality he locates at the beginning of human life is uncertain. This is because it is understood only as a moment of absolute consciousness or the absolute concept that is at least implicitly rational is all its forms. Even if Hegel does recognize an authentic irrationality at the beginning of human development he argues that this irrationality is dialectically and therefore irreversibly overcome by reason. This is evident in his account of desire.

Desire arises as a result of the original split of self-consciousness. The particular objects of desire, however, are determined by the structure of ends and incentives established by reason or spirit in the social world. The historical development of this world culminates in the rational state in which desire is directed toward the most rational object, that is, toward freedom. This does not mean that other objects are not desired but that the desire, for example, for food and sex, is not an end in itself but is subordinate to the desire for freedom. Whether desire can be directed and restrained in this manner, however, is far from clear.

In the first place, it is possible that desire is not the simple response to the alienation of self-consciousness. It may be a response to appetites that naturally and unchangeably aim at particular objects. If this is the case, as the ancients believed, then it may not be as easy to redirect desire as Hegel assumed. It may be possible to direct certain desires such as the desire for physical pleasure or honor to somewhat more rational or less degenerate ends, but this may not be the case for the perverse or predatory desires that aim at total mastery and universal degradation. A just and stable political order may always depend upon the suppression or repression of certain desires and thus upon an irremediable frustration of some human impulses, as such diverse thinkers as Locke and Freud have pointed out. Hegel thought that such desires are characteristic of only the most primitive forms of consciousness and that they do not motivate modern men. Therefore, he saw little need to establish safeguards against them.

In this respect Hegel stands in opposition to Plato and Aristotle who repeatedly argue that man can fall below nature as well as rise above it, that the tyrant in other words is equally if not more likely than the philospher. Hegel recognized the danger of a tyranny of freedom, such as that of the French Revolution, but he saw this as the result of idealistic and disinterested motives rather than tyrannical desires. In fact with the possible exception of the oriental despot at the beginning of history, the figure of the tyrant disappears altogether in Hegel's thought in favor of the world-historical individual who is motivated by desire but whose desire is always in the service of reason. If our age has learned anything, however, it is man's continued capacity for a tyrannical bestiality that reason cannot explain and that history cannot excuse.

The belief in the triumph of reason also seems to lie at the heart of Hegel's assumption that all ideological disagreement and conflict had come to an end. He knew, perhaps more fully than anyone else, the extent to which history itself was a continual debate about the nature of truth and reason. His *Phenomenology* is the recollection and representation of this debate. Hegel, however, also believed he had demonstrated that this debate had come to its end in his thought. Thus, all that was necessary to secure the rule of reason was to embody the principles he had discovered in institutions. The rational state was the primary vehicle by which he believed this rule would be brought about.

Hegel also recognized the danger posed to the rule of reason by the irrationality of romanticism and especially by the romantic nationalism of Fries and others, which later manifested itself in National Socialism.[49] It is thus surprising that he had so little inkling of the ideological debates of the nineteenth and twentieth centuries. He also did not foresee the rise of nihilism and existentialism. Indeed, he believed he had explicitly solved this problem.[50] The consequences of this optimism for politics were ominous.

Modern liberals have often pointed out the dangers of ideological fanaticism for political life. They argue that moderation and freedom are dependent upon institutional safeguards that prevent fanaticism from either coming to power or using the state administration to secure its ends. Hegel argued that this sort of ideological fanaticism had come to an end with the advent of absolute knowledge and the embodiment of this knowledge in the institutions of the rational state. The structure of incentive and the system of education in this state would effectively form the character of the bureaucratic or universal class by instilling in them the correct notions of justice and right. Checks on bureaucratic power were thus unnecessary. Indeed, where reason ruled it would be improper to give way to interests and desires as every system of checks and balances does. Interests and desires must be taken into account in determining the rational interest of the community, but the state should lead public opinion rather than follow it.[51] Unfortunately, a state that is responsive to rational administration is also responsive to irrational administration. The rational state aims at restraining bourgeois society and correcting its inequitites, and it tolerates cultural and racial differences. The irrational state seeks to destroy society and extinguish differences. Our century has all too often witnessed the ravages wrought by fanaticism that has gained control of the state administration and used it in the service of ideological ends. It would be incorrect to assert that Hegel did not recognize such dangers. He did, however, believe that they had been overcome in part because he thought that war would restrain both bourgeoisification and irrationality.

War, for Hegel, draws men beyond self-interest to a concern for the general good of the state. It thus also measures the respective rationality of states. World history is the world judge. Hegel assumed that the superior strength of a state resides in its superior rationality, that is, in the perfection of the harmony it establishes between individual desire and the general good. But is such a state the most powerful? One has to wonder whether bourgeois habits and tastes do not undermine the spiritedness and martial virtue necessary in war. While a professional army can partially remedy this problem, it is not sufficient, for as Hegel admits, the state will at times have to depend upon all of its citizens to fight in its defense. Indeed, if states were not brought to such extremes, war would not pose a real danger to them and would not restrain bourgeois society in the way Hegel desired. Such citizen soldiers, however, are likely to be inferior to the troops of a state in which ideological imperatives have suppressed individualism. Hegel admitted that the strength of the state in war depends upon the spiritual courage and attachment of the citizens to the state, but he felt that this courage would be most highly developed in the citizen who saw the state as the basis of his individual freedom and self-interest. We, however, who have seen the strength of the irrational appeal to abandon individual freedom and self-interest and have witnessed the awful effectiveness of these ideological armies cannot be as sanguine as Hegel. As a result, we must doubt his assertion that the rational state is the strongest of all possible states. We must therefore also doubt that the rational state will come to be or, coming to be, that it will survive.

Even if we grant the superior strength of the rational state, we still cannot accept Hegel's notion of war as the regulative restraint of bourgeois society because of the disastrous development of war itself. Hegel assumed that wars would become increasingly more humane, but this has not happened. Instead, wars have become more horrible than anything he imagined, so horrible in the case of nuclear war that no sane man can argue that it could have the salutary effect for politics and human life that Hegel supposed. This failure to foresee the development of modern warfare seems to invalidate Hegel's notion of war as a restraint on bourgeoisification and thus to call into question the adequacy of his understanding of the role of death in defining the character of human life. Such a conclusion, however, goes too far and obscures the profundity of Hegel's thought and its crucial meaning for us today.

Let us assume that Hegel's analysis of the role of war in restraining bourgeois life is correct and that the development of modern warfare has made such a restraint impossible. What follows? We might expect to see the triumph of bourgeois society and a universal hedonism slowly but surely undermining all institutions of freedom. This would draw man away from the community into an unrestrained pursuit of his own self-interest.

This would only be the case if war were removed altogether as a possibility. But war has become an even greater danger than it was in Hegel's time, and it poses an even greater threat to man, since every individual is threatened with annihilation. Does this threat lift man above his own self-interest in the way Hegel assumed war would? This seems unlikely since individual self-sacrifice is meaningless in this situation. The possibility of such a war seems to leave man isolated and alone. Not only does this undermine the effect of war in restraining bourgeois life but it exacerbates the individualism at its heart. Man is thus plunged into schizophrenia: one moment he forgets death entirely and is concerned only with his present pleasure and advantage; the next moment he recognizes its imminence and dedicates himself to abolishing the weapons that make it possible. His lack of success leads him to recognize that he is not the master of his fate. Rather, he and all his fellows are mastered by an inexplicable and irresistable necessity that—in the looming form of death—propels them into a frenzied accumulation of the means of destruction they most want to destroy. The threat of nuclear war thus seems not only to remove the check upon desire that in Hegel's view war establishes but to augment this desire by continually confronting us with the imminence of death.

If these speculations are not sufficiently disheartening, one has only to note the increased likelihood of war as a result of the triumph of bourgeois society over state authority. Under such circumstances we can only hope that Hegel's analysis is wrong or that he is right on a deeper level, that the same conditions that propel us toward disaster will also give birth to a new way of philosophizing that will yet prove to be our solace and our salvation.

Notes

1. Jean Hyppolite, *Genesis and Structure of Hegel's Phenomenology of Spirit*, trans. Samuel Cherneak and John Heckman (Evanston: Northwestern University Press, 1974), 160.
2. George Wilhelm Friedrich Hegel, *Die Phänomenologie des Geistes*, in *Werke in Zwanzig Bänden*, ed. Eva Moldenhauer and Karl Markus Michel (Frankfurt: Suhrkamp, 1970–71), 3:24 (hereafter cited as *Ph*); Hegel, *Jenenser Realphilosophie*, ed. Johannes Hoffmeister, 2 vols. (Leipzig: Meiner, 1931–32), 2:209 (hereafter cited as *RP*); see also Hyppolite, *Genesis*, 164.
3. See Hyppolite, *Genesis*, 163–64 for a fuller discussion of this point.
4. *RP*, 2:207.
5. Ibid., 205.
6. Hegel, *Geschichte der Philosophie*, in *Werke*, 19:108. Plamenatz and others who have assumed that this is a struggle for physical predominance go astray here. John Plamenatz, *Man and Society*, 2 vols. (New York: McGraw-Hill, 1963), 2:188–89. On this matter Hegel follows not Homer but Hobbes and, more importantly, Locke.
7. *RP*, 2:206.
8. Plamenatz, *Man and Society*, 2:153.
9. It is here that Kojève goes astray in his attempt to transform the *Phenomenology* into a philsophy of history. Alexandre Kojève, *Introduction à la lecture de Hegel* (Paris: Gallimard, 1947). While Kojève's interpretation does highlight one aspect of Hegel's argument, his failure to recognize the logical and psychological

sides of the work leads to a fundamental distortion in his interpretation.

10. This view has been thoughtfully argued by George Armstrong Kelly in his "Notes on Hegel's 'Lordship and Bondage,' " *Review of Metaphysics* 19, no. 4 (June 1966):784, 788–89.

11. Ibid., 785, 796–99. Kelly insightfully shows that Hegel's location of this struggle within self-consciousness is a rejection of Fichte's and Schelling's theory of two primordial races who embodied these antagonistic elements. Hegel thus avoids the racist conclusion that Romanticism is often driven to espouse.

12. Hyppolite, *Genesis*, 169.

13. *RP*, 1:228; see also Kojève, *Introduction*, 564–65.

14. *RP*, 2:211; Hegel, *Grundlinien der Philosophie des Rechts oder Naturrecht und Staatswissenschaft im Grundrisse*, in *Werke*, 7:51 (hereafter cited as *PR*).

15. *RP*, 227; Hegel, *Enzyklopädie der philosophischen Wissenschaften im Grundrisse*, 10:220 (hereafter cited as *E*).

16. *E*, 10:225; see also Hyppolite, *Genesis*, 173.

17. Hegel, *Vorlesungen über die Philosophie der Geschichte*, in *Werke*, 12:225 (hereafter cited as *PG*).

18. Kelly, "Notes," 792. Kelly shows quite clearly that this section of Hegel's work and indeed the *Phenomenology* as a whole often accept an inherently Platonic psychology.

19. See Kojève, *Introduction*, 572.

20. Hegel, *Die Verfassung Deutschlands*, in *Werke*, 1:597 (hereafter cited as *VD*).

21. *E*, 10:220–21.

22. *VD*, 1:608; *GP*, 19:108.

23. *PR*, 7:507.

24. See Kelly, "Notes," 784, 799.

25. See Hyppolite, *Genesis*, 174, 177. His error on this point reflects his underlying intention to push Hegel in the direction of Marx. Kojève correctly sees history as a reconciliation of master and slave but goes astray in supposing that Napoleon's citizen-soldiers represent the resolution of this struggle for Hegel. Kojève, *Introduction*, 559.

26. Hegel, *Philosophie des Rechts: Die Vorlesung von 1819/20 in einer Nachschrift*, ed. Dieter Henrich (Frankfurt a.M.: Suhrkamp, 1983), 275 (hereafter cited as *PR 1819/20*).

27. *PR*, 7:493.

28. *PR 1819/20*, 276.

29. *RP*, 2:258n. Hegel argues here in fact that duels must be allowed among soldiers to avoid weakening their sense of personal honor.

30. *PR*, 7:496; see also Shlomo Avineri, "The Problem of War in Hegel's Thought," *Journal of the History of Ideas* 22 (1961):470.

31. *PR 1819/20*, 277; *PR*, 7:497.

32. *PR*, 7:502.

33. Ibid.

34. *VD*, 1:539.

35. *PR*, 7:491–94.

36. See Avineri, "The Problem of War," 420.

37. *PR*, 7:494.

38. *VD*, 1:541; see also Shlomo Avineri, *Hegel's Theory of the Modern State* (Cambridge: Cambridge University Press, 1972), 196.

39. This argument is also a justification of colonialism. *PG*, 12:125–26. Whether colonialism is justified if it aims at mere economic advantage and ceases to act as an agent of rational change, however, seems unlikely.

40. This was nowhere so clear for Hegel as in his own native Germany, which had been crushed by the French when he was a young man, prompting him to proclaim in an early unpublished work, "Germany is no longer a state" (*VD*, 1:472–73). Indeed his thought as a whole can be understood as an attempt to find a new basis for German political life.

41. *VD*, 1:486, 491, 503.

42. Hegel, *Differenz des Fischteschen und Schellingschen Systems der Philosophie*, in *Werke*, 2:20–25.

43. See Judith Shklar, "Hegel's *Phenomenology*: an Elegy for Hellas," in *Hegel's Political Philosophy: Problems and Perspectives*, ed. Z. A. Pelczynski (Cambridge: Cambridge University Press, 1971), 73–89.

44. This interpretation has been defended by Karl Popper, *The Open Society and its Enemies*, 4th ed., 2 vols. (Princeton: Princeton University Press, 1963); Sidney Hook, "Hegel Habilitated?" *Encounter* 24 (January 1965):53–58; and Hubert Kieswetter, *Von Hegel zu Hitler: Eine Analyse der Hegelschen Machtstaatideologie und der politischen Wirkungsgeschichte des Rechtshegelianismus* (Hamburg: Hoffman und Campe, 1974).

45. It is thus only partially correct to maintain that Hegel merely describes the actuality of war. For this view see Avineri, "Problem

of War," 473; Constance Smith, "Hegel on War," *Journal of the History of Ideas* 26 (1965):282–85; and H. G. ten Bruggencate, "Hegel's Views on War," *Philosophical Quarterly* 1 (1950):59. Hegel points rather to the future, to what war is likely to become.

46. While the general tenor of Hegel's work reflects such optimism, one is occasionally struck by his apparent recognition of the imminent collapse of rationality and the triumph of nihilism. His assertion in the preface to the *Philosophy of Right* that "the owl of Minerva takes wing only at dusk" is indicative of this point of view (*PR*, 7:28). Such statements, however, are rare and do not counterbalance his repeated assertions that reason rules the world.

47. Such an existential interpretation was developed and defended by Alexandre Koyré and Jean Wahl among others. See Alexandre Koyré, "Rapport sur l'état des études hegelien en France," in *Verhandlung des ersten Hegelkongresses vom 22. bis 25. April 1930 im Haag*, ed. Baltus Wigersma (Tubingen: Mohr, 1931, Haarlem: Willinz, 1931), 80–105; and Jean Wahl, *Le Malheur de la conscience dans la philosophie de Hegel*, 2d ed. (Paris: Presses Universitaires de France, 1951).

48. On the problem of the logical ground of Hegel's thought see my *Hegel, Heidegger, and the Ground of History* (Chicago: University of Chicago Press, 1984), 96–103, 113–15.

49. *PR*, 7:17–20.

50. Hegel, "Glauben und Wissen," in *Werke*, 2:430–33.

51. *PR*, 7:486.

WERNER
DANNHAUSER

X

Spiritedness in
Thus Spoke Zarathustra

Whatever else spiritedness may be, it is surely difficult to define. Good teachers like Joseph Cropsey[1] wisely tell us that a good part of wisdom consists of working toward the definition of significant terms instead of beginning with them, but we do want to "find a handle" for a fruitful progress of inquiry. To put it more simply, we need a preliminary answer to a legitimate question: What are we talking about when we speak of spiritedness?

For present purposes, a beguilingly simple answer suggests itself. By spiritedness we mean primarily, though perhaps not exclusively, what Plato means by *thymos* in *The Republic*. Therefore, when trying to understand Nietzsche's view of spiritedness in *Thus Spoke Zarathustra*, we can begin with the German word for the Greek word *thymos*.

At this point, our difficulties begin, though most of them present no insuperable obstacles. Nietzsche, a professor of classical philology for a number of years, had no need to resort to any translation of the term *thymos*; he enjoyed reading the Greek classics in Greek.[2] He has, however, next to nothing to say about the term *thymos* itself.[3] Yet Nietzsche is surely a philosopher and as such concerned with the whole of things, especially the human part of the whole. Whatever else spiritedness as thymos may be, it is surely an estimable part of the human part of the whole; it is therefore a pheonomenon Nietzsche must have addressed in one way or another.

We can well suppose that thymos crept into German philosophical usage by way of a translation. In the nineteenth century,
Plato had found a German translator of unusual competence and
high standards of literalness, Schleiermacher, whose translation
of *The Republic* enjoyed both popularity and authority. Nietzsche
knew Schleiermacher's work as translator and writer; moreover,
he probably owned a copy of his translations.[4] Perhaps he used
Schleiermacher's translation of thymos.

Surprisingly enough, Schleiermacher renders thymos as
Eifer, the German for "zeal." We thus learn something of the
enigmatic quality of the term. In discussing spiritedness and
thymos, scholars most often refer to *anger*, *nobility*, and *indignation*, and *zeal* does not at once remind us of those reasonable
equivalents. *Eifer* can come close to "fervor," but in everyday
German it means little more than eagerness or industriousness.
For example, we refer to the eagerness of schoolchildren to learn
as their *Eifer*. Did Schleiermacher assimilate Plato to modern
rationalism as was the tendency of the time, by rendering thymos
a bit more softly than others would?

Our task is not to answer that question but to find out
what Nietzsche had to say about *Eifer*. What is more, the
Nietzsche indices are probably right in suggesting that he had
nothing to say. We might suspect as much from the fact that in
German *Eifer* is part of *Eifersucht*, which means "jealousy" and
can be rendered as "addition to zeal." Various plays on words
suggest themselves, and this use of *Eifer* would be one of those
rare cases on record when Nietzsche did not seize an opportunity
for verbal play. (Incidentally, both Schleiermacher and Goethe
rose to the occasion.)[5]

Eifer can be found in the works of Nietzsche, but it is a
common enough word that we would have to explain its absence
rather than its presence. It is more to the point that in *Thus Spoke
Zarathustra* the word *Eifer* is used with extreme casualness, and
primarily in part IV of the book, the part about which it can be
argued whether it is integral to Nietzsche's magnum opus.[6] In
one of those adventures that would be bizarre for ordinary hu-

man beings, Zarathustra passes some cows who seem to be listening *mit Eifer* (eagerly) to a speaker. Hearing a human voice in the midst of the herd and fearing that somebody may have been hurt, Zarathustra jumps up *mit Eifer* and pushes the animals apart. His fears prove unfounded, for the man, the "voluntary beggar" after whom the speech is named, has suffered no harm.[7] The use of the term *Eifer* in connection with the incident offers no occasion or need for interpretation in depth. Nietzsche treats neither thymos nor *Eifer* in his work, so our investigation has reached a dead end.

We are forced to begin again, to pursue a new line of inquiry. If we were asked to render spiritedness in German, what would we say? Moreover, what term does Nietzsche use when discussing the phenomena *The Republic* treats under the rubric of thymos? In answer to both of these questions no better word comes up than *Mut*. The leading dictionaries lend their support to this translation, though the most obvious and primary English equivalent of *Mut* is "courage." That need not deter us, if only because of the intimate connection in *The Republic* between thymos and courage. In that book the three-part division of the soul parallels the three-part division of the polis. Thymos issues from the part of the soul paralleled by the soldiers of *The Republic*, whose special attribute is obviously courage.[8]

Mut can also mean "mood," as the phonetic closeness of those two words suggests. This secondary meaning aids our investigation; for the mood that we have or suffer depends on how spirited or dis-spirited we are; mood is inseparable from spiritedness.

The richness of the term *Mut* in German depends in part on a noteworthy characteristic of the German language: we can put almost anything in front of those three letters and fashion a word that no longer obviously refers to courage. For example, *Armut* means "poverty."[9] A number of things can also be added to *Mut* to make different words. Nietzsche, almost obsessively playful with the German language, does both, as shown below.

New words also take on a life of their own in the English

language (though to an appreciably lesser extent than in German), so that we forget their derivation. Thus, when we speak of discouraging somebody, we do not usually remember that to discourage has something—almost everything—to do with taking away courage. Similarly, when we *encourage* somebody, we try to give him courage. We usually forget to think of it that way. One of the many useful tasks performed by poets and philosophers is to remind us of basic truths by way of making clear the genius of language. In his incomparably elegant and eloquent way, Nietzsche teaches us about the varieties of courage and of spiritedness.

The beginning of *Thus Spoke Zarathustra* surprises us by manifesting no special interest in courage. The fact that it has a great deal to say about virtue in general legitimates our surprise. We could suppose that Nietzsche's analysis moves from virtue in general to specific virtues, and that proves to be correct overall, but it does not explain everything. "Zarathustra's Prologue" dwells on virtue as such and its relation to reason and happiness, but the prologue mentions wisdom and not courage.[10]

We come closer to an explanation when we realize that in Nietzsche's scheme destructiveness must precede constructiveness and play an integral part in it. Zarathustra finds no need and little occasion to speak of courage while performing his necessary task of destruction because he has nothing destructive to say about courage, at least when courage is compared or contrasted with other virtues.[11]

An even more plausible explanation suggests itself: *Thus Spoke Zarathustra* begins with a critique of traditional morality, with the virtues and vices as conventionally understood by "the good and the just."[12] In terms of both nineteenth-century Europe and Nietzsche's view, conventional morality means Christian morality. Whatever we could say about Christian morality, we would be hard put to say that it assigns a prominent or preeminent place to courage. Since Nietzsche's Zarathustra begins by tearing down Christian morality, he naturally has little to say at first about courage.[13]

This should not be taken to suggest that what the prologue and book I have to say about virtue in general is useless in our attempt to understand courage or spiritedness in *Thus Spoke Zarathustra*. The second speech of book I, "On the Chairs of Virtue," proves instructive. In that speech, a boring teacher propounds a tepid teaching about virtues and makes the students sleepy. Thus, we learn something of Nietzsche's task: to inspirit the virtues and supplement them with spiritedness; moreover, we discover that one has to draw limits to the virtues. Virtues are jealous of each other; each particular virtue wishes to reign supreme and pass for the whole of virtue; in Zarathustra's universe one virtue is worth more than two virtues.[14] The book clearly announces a contest, an agon among virtues, and one soon suspects that the victor will be courage.

The emergence and triumph of courage comes about gradually in *Thus Spoke Zarathustra*. In fact, the speeches of part I contain a reference to *Hochmut* ("arrogance" or literally "high courage") before mentioning *Mut*, courage proper.[15] Only a passing reference is made to *Mut* in the chapter "On War and Warriors," where Zarathustra asserts that "war and courage" have accomplished greater things than love of one's neighbor.[16] But the explanation for this semi-silence proves simple: for strictly martial virtue Nietzsche uses the word *Tapferkeit*, which translates as "bravery" or "valor," though he does so inconsistently. It makes rough sense to use a special word for the courage of soldiers, for if we equate their excellence with courage simply, we must, as one does in English, talk almost at once about phenomena like "civil courage."

The first sustained reference to courage as such, not bravery, occurs in the speech "On Reading and Writing," the seventh speech in part I. In that speech, Zarathustra mocks the usual writing and reading of the time—our time—for being heavy-footed, clumsy, tedious, at once too serious and not serious enough. As an alternative he praises writing in "blood and maxims," the words of those who wish and deserve to be "learned by heart," rather than read. Maxims resemble mountain peaks, and their author must know how to live in rarefied air, must possess a spirit full of "gay malice." Zarathustra is such a man; he states, "I want to have goblins around me for I am courageous (*mutig*). Courage (*Mut*) that puts ghosts to flight creates goblins for itself: courage wishes to laugh." Shortly thereafter, Zarathustra proclaims, "courageous, unconcerned, mocking, violent—thus wisdom wants us: she is woman and always loves only a warrior."[17]

Great writing and wise reading, then, require a combination of verve and nerve, a kind of spiritedness Nietzsche calls courage. (This notion of courage should encourage all those who specialize in turning to the pen rather than the sword.) We notice at once that courage is not simply a moral virtue, and Nietzsche will make that abundantly clear later on in *Thus Spoke Zarathustra*.

Zarathustra remains relatively silent about courage while dwelling on the social dimension of virtue in general, thus preparing us for a different and differing appreciation of it. Nietzsche gives virtue its due because of the low but solid ground of its usefulness to society. If human beings are to live together with the requisite amount of concern, certain rules must be obeyed, certain characteristics cultivated, certain dispositions honored. One needs virtues for the sake of political life. Ordinary courage is of such utility: unless a goodly number of citizens prefer death to dishonor, their country cannot survive. The survival of the group demands the willingness of individuals to die for their country.

Zarathustra recognizes but ultimately disdains the utilitarian argument for virtue in general and for courage in particular. Zarathustra's talk of *Mut* increases as his contact with mankind decreases. In the prologue, he attempts to persuade the many of mankind's need to transcend itself by producing the superman. He fails miserably. Thereupon, in part I, he confines himself to educating and exhorting a group of disciples in a town called the Motley Cow. In part II, he returns to the task of spreading and defending his teaching, but this time he chooses a more

exclusive locale, and presumably a more select audience, on the
Blessed Isles. He bids farewell to these disciples as well and, in
book III, returns to his lonely mountain top. He now talks mostly
to himself, fully aware of the dangers and problems of such an
endeavor.[18]

In setting the stage for the discussion of courage in part III
of *Thus Spoke Zarathustra*, we must plot the development of the
argument in regard to virtue. For the sake of brevity we have
to schematize rather ruthlessly and thus be less than perfectly
faithful to the complexities of the book.

Zarathustra understands himself as a man whose task consists of nothing less than revaluation and transvaluation of all
virtues. Traditional virtue requires transvaluation because the
death of God has rendered it groundless, baseless, and arbitrary.
With the death of God, man must cease to be man, having
previously been constituted by his faith in God and by the virtues
depending on the existence of God. It had been thought, for
example, that a man owed his fellow man a good deal simply
because he was a child of God. Traditional teachings of virtue
base themselves on the existence of God (or at least on the existence of transcendent standards), viewing all human beings as
equally creative, equally sinful (or at least deficient when judged
by transcendent standards).

With the death of God, man must necessarily become more
than he has been, the superman, or less, the last man.[19] The
superman will need new virtues, for the old have been discred-
ited. They have aimed at rendering man a useful member of the
herd rather than a unique self and have wrongly emphasized
parsimony, a bourgeois pettiness, at the expense of extravagance
or extravagant squandering. And they have diminished human
beings rather than encouraged them to become who they are.[20]
Zarathustra attempts to provide humanity with new tablets of
morality, which, to be sure, can only be half-finished, since the
uniqueness of the unique self sets limits to the general rules it
can be expected to follow.[21]

Zarathustra provides us with numerous examples of the

revaluation and transvaluation he effects or half-effects. In the first speech of part II, he transforms wisdom into "wild wisdom," freeing it from the niggardly constraints of logic and the kind of argumentation that shuns contradiction and makes a fetish of consistency. Zarathustra's wild wisdom is no longer what philosophers have traditionally loved or possessed. Indeed, it resembles poetry more than it resembles traditional philosophy.[22]

Justice is revalued so that its traditional emphasis on equality yields to a new emphasis on hierarchy, rank order, and the inequality of everything.[23]

Apparently, moderation resists all attempts to transvalue it. Transvaluation involves radicalization, and a radicalized moderation ceases to be moderation. Therefore Zarathustra simply dismisses it with yet another play on words. He stresses the closeness of moderation, *Mässigkeit*, to mediocrity, *Mittelmässigkeit*.[24]

A number of other virtues undergo a similar treatment at the hands of Zarathustra; for example, prudence is transfigured almost beyond recognition.[25] We have, however, deliberately restricted the evidence to the four cardinal virtues and now turn to the missing one.

What of courage? Perhaps it stands in no need of revaluation or transvaluation because it lacks nothing and requires no enhancement. We can argue that nothing needs fixing here because Zarathustra never has any fault to find with courage. He does not find it contemptible nor has he a bad word for it.

Nevertheless, one can readily see that courage profits from adornment. Nietzsche's terminology leads one gently to the conclusion that courage, *Mut*, can be enhanced by becoming *Anmut*, which is a kind of graciousness or gracefulness, and ultimately *Grossmut*, literally great courage, which means great-souledness or magnanimity. Zarathustra connects these terms in a speech entitled "On Those Who Are Sublime," which is devoted to the elevation of human beings to the truly beautiful.[26]

We cannot, however, leave it at the need for the mere

adornment of courage. Zarathustra must effect a real transvaluation of courage because courage has too many ties to the spirit
of revenge and to the spirit of gravity that he dedicates himself
to vanquishing.[27]

Courage is akin to the will to power because it almost
always entails overcoming. A soldier devotes himself to overcoming the enemy without and the fear of death within. Overcoming turns out to be steady work because things resist being
overcome. Recalcitrance characterizes both the external and internal enemies that courage confronts.

The world is such that it calls for courage, but it also limits
the range of courage. Apparently, no way exists to overcome
time and its ravages, it being in the nature of time to pass.[28] In
time, all human beings die; time mocks all human aspirations
and turns all the works of man to dust.

In the face of time's harsh sovereignty, courage can come
to display a bitter kind of railing. It breeds resentment at what
it fails to overcome. The courageous man then resembles somebody who beats his head against unyielding walls.

Nietzsche has a number of terms to describe the curdlings
of courage. *Mut*, courage, too easily turns into *Schwermut*,
literally heavy courage, which means melancholy.[29] Or it can
decline into *Unmut*, which can mean anything from discouragement to grumpiness and disgruntlement. In discouragement,
gnawing worms parasitically degenerate the high into the low.[30]
Nietzsche's playful use of words as he treats of the damages to
courage should not blind us to the fact that he thinks courage is
always needed and that in *Thus Spoke Zarathustra* the need for
it continues and intensifies as the argument develops.[31]

For the last time, we must resort to over-schematization
and recapitulate the development of the argument in *Thus Spoke
Zarathustra*. In the first part of the book, Zarathustra concerns
himself primarily with the consequence of the death of God, the
major consequence being that man can and must cease to be man
and become superman. In the second part of the book, we find
the articulation of Nietzsche's doctrine of the will to power.

Zarathustra's discovery—or creation—of that doctrine at once reveals the deep problems connected with the will to power. Man could be the animal who can will anything, but no God or transcendent standard exists any longer to guide him in his willing. Moreover, the irrevocable, inexorable passing of time mocks man's power of willing, his will to power.

In response to these and kindred problems, the third part of *Thus Spoke Zarathustra* becomes necessary so that Zarathustra can will the eternal recurrence of the same. Man compensates for the death of God by affirming all, by saying yes to the world as it is. He finds a worthy goal in the consecration of the world, no longer having any need of otherworldly aspirations. Moreover, if all things recur infinitely, man will be able to will the past by willing the future; man will be able to become the cause of himself. The grim turn courage took can be transfigured. Thinking such profound, not to say unfathomable, thoughts, Zarathustra finds himself, to repeat, in solitude.

Courage soon comes to the fore and Zarathustra's praise of it reaches a climax. The second speech of part III is entitled "On The Vision and The Riddle," and it refers to Zarathustra's enigmatic vision of the eternal return of the same. In order to live up to the awesome task of willing the eternal return of the same, Zarathustra must summon up his courage to combat the spirit of gravity (a dwarf), the gloom that weighs him down, the despondency that keeps him from total affirmation. He therefore says:

> But there is something in me that I call courage: that has so far slain my every discouragement. This courage finally bade me stand still and speak: "Dwarf! it is you or I!"
>
> For courage is the best slayer, courage which *attacks*; for in every attack there is playing and brass.
>
> Man, however, is the most courageous animal, hence he overcomes every animal. With playing and brass he has so far overcome every pain; but human pain is the deepest pain.
>
> Courage also slays dizziness at the edge of abysses:

and where does man not stand at the edge of abysses?
Is not seeing always seeing abysses?
    Courage is the best slayer: courage slays even pity.
But pity is the deepest abyss: as deeply as man sees
into life, he also sees into suffering.
    Courage, however, is the best slayer—courage
which attacks, which slays even death itself, for it
says: "Was *that* life? Well, then! Once more!"[32]

The above passage deserves detailed explication, but for
our purposes two comments will provide sufficient exegesis.

First of all, we should notice that at this juncture courage
or spiritedness has been magnified to such an extent that it has
become almost synonymous with the will to power itself. For
example, courage here gets credit for man's overcoming man's
animality and thus becoming man. It will presumably also get
credit for man's overcoming his humanity to become superman.
Nietzsche more often writes of the will to power in such terms.

Second, on the basis of this passage, we can state categor-
ically what we have previously only suggested. Courage is all
important because it is not only a moral virtue but also an intellectual one. Courage is the quality of mind most needed by
the mind as it faces the utter and comprehensive meaninglessness
of life. That meaninglessness must be affirmed, lest the spirit of
revenge corrode us and we face a hostile world with bitterness
and resentment. In fact, most meaninglessness must be willed,
for when we will the eternal return of the same we will the most
meaningless of all possible universes, a world in which everything happens again and again and again without rhyme or reason. Man needs courage to face the truth—to pursue it—when
the truth has ceased to be beautiful. Truth may be a woman[33]
but that woman may be old and gnarled and ugly.[34]

The fact that courage as such is praised does not mean that
courage cannot undergo transvaluation. Once more we turn to
Nietzsche's use of words as a way of instructing ourselves.

The transvaluation of man means that man becomes superman; *Mensch* becomes *Übermensch*. *Thus Spoke Zarathustra* is

loaded, perhaps overloaded, with terms to which Nietzsche prefixes the words *über* or *unter*, over (or super-) and under (or sub-).[35] Is there, then, an over-courage or a super-courage? There is, indeed.

Übermut, literally super-courage or over-courage, is one of those words which, in German, has assumed a life of its own, as it were, so much in daily usage that it is not always connected with courage. It means playfulness or even prankishness. Zarathustra uses it almost interchangeably with *Mutwille*, literally courage-will, which can mean mischievousness, wantonness and petulance.

Mischievous playfulness is, in a certain way, what Zarathustra has in mind for mankind's future. Men have been camels, beasts bearing the burdens of moral obligation. With the death of God, they become lions, destructively exercising their will. But while lions use their will, they lack positive goals, and thus they become nihilists. The final metamorphosis of the spirit means that man must become a child. Children play games without bothering, or having to bother, about the meaning—or meaninglessness—of what they do. Their play confutes the spirit of gravity in speech and refutes it in deed.[36]

Zarathustra bestows lavish praise on *Übermut* and *Mutwille*, on playfulness and prankishness, in the third part of *Thus Spoke Zarathustra*. He celebrates the strength required for them once he has attained that strength. Super-courage takes the place of mundane rationality; and in a song on the Mount of Olives, Zarathustra substitutes prankishness for grave piety.[37]

Zarathustra's exuberance after his willing of the eternal return reaches its peak in "The Other Dancing Song." The title alludes to a dancing song in part II, in which life had mocked and bested Zarathustra. Now, however, Zarathustra has become the equal of life, whose lover he prides himself on being. Having understood the eternal return of the same, he has understood life. As the lover of life he can address it in endearing terms. In this song, Zarathustra lovingly calls life a prankster—an *Übermut*.[38]

Courage gives way to super-courage; the higher playfulness vanquishes the spirit of gravity; the will to power persists
even in its overcoming of itself; bliss attends one's willing of the
eternal return of the same as one takes the world with a sense
of acceptance and even gratitude—and yet *Thus Spoke Zarathustra*
ultimately educes more sadness than triumphant affirmation.

That feeling owes a good deal to the realization the book
forces on us that the note of triumph that attends overcoming
sounds for one moment only. Then time does its work and we
must gird ourselves for the next task. In one way, therefore, the
book simply reinforces an experience many of us have had with
courage. We beat up the bully, or defend the good cause, and
then think we have conquered our cowardice and that henceforth
we will be steadily courageous. The next day it turns out that
not much has changed. The bully instills fear; one has a sickening
urge to abandon the good cause: one is a coward again.

In the fourth and final part of *Thus Spoke Zarathustra*, Zarathustra experiences a noon of happiness when "the world is
perfect." But noon precedes afternoon and heralds night; time
passes.[39] The whole of the last part buttresses this insight. By
this time, presumably, Zarathustra has attained the rank of superman, and a superman is somebody who has conquered the human—all too human—feelings of pity that divert an ordinary
man from his great tasks. Yet Zarathustra must continue to resist
the temptations that pity exerts.

In general, we can say that the tone of book IV of *Thus
Spoke Zarathustra* comes across as more muted and subdued than
we might expect as sequel to Zarathustra's glorious willing of
the eternal return of the same. For example it contains a poem
about "heavy courage," *Schwermut*, melancholy, a "Song of Melancholy" in a chapter bearing that title.[40] We can argue that the
song is sung not by Zarathustra but by one of the quaint "higher
men" of the final part, the magician. That does not explain,
however, Nietzsche's willingness to sing substantially the same
song in his own name, in the "Dionysian Dithyrambs."[41]

Courage surely receives its due in the whole of *Thus Spoke
Zarathustra*. The philosophic tradition may have done less than

perfect justice to spiritedness, but in Nietzsche's work it comes into its own.

The trouble is that it comes into its own with a vengeance. Nietzsche's human world, in the end, seems to contain *only* spiritedness, except perhaps for the deadly and deadening sloth that characterizes the last man.

The spiritedness that combats sloth, in turn, turns out to be increasingly difficult to distinguish from energy without focus, from frenzy. It has no aim in view, no goal it can set itself. It lacks dignity for the things that would dignify it even while limiting it—Nietzsche has denied the existence of all such things. Courage may account for the whole prehistory of man,[42] but when it comes into its own there is no real ground for rejoicing.

No wonder, then, that one of the last comments Zarathustra makes about courage compares it to looking into the abyss with pride.[43] Time keeps on passing, and the abyss keeps on confronting man, for whom spiritedness brings no happiness.

Notes

1. My debts to Joseph Cropsey go beyond the possibility of specific acknowledgment in footnotes, as does my indebtedness to our common teacher, Leo Strauss.

2. The details of Nietzsche's classical training can be found in Richard Blunck, *Friedrich Nietzsche: Kindheit und Jugend* (Basel: Ernst Reinhardt Verlag, 1953).

3. The index on which I have drawn most extensively is by Karl Schlechta, *Nietzsche Index zu den Werken in Drei Banden* (Munich: Carl Hanser Verlag, 1965). However, I also consulted the indices to a number of other editions—with identical results.

4. All references to Nietzsche in German will be to the edition edited by Karl Schlechta, *Nietzsche: Werke in Drei Banden* (Munich: Carl Hanser Verlag, 1954–1956). For Nietzsche's familiarity with Schleiermacher, consider vol. I, pp. 164, 193, 268, 532, 965, 1137; vol. II, p. 1149.

5. German has an eerie saying for which both are given credit: *Eifersucht ist die Leidenschuft die mit Eifer sucht was Leiden schafft.* It literally

means "Jealousy is the passion that zealously seeks what causes suffering," but is a multiple and untranslatable pun.

6. The necessary philological information can be found in Schlechta, op. cit. vol. III, pp. 1373–76.

7. Ibid., vol. II, p. 506 in the speech, "The Voluntary Beggar." All references to *Thus Spoke Zarathustra* will be the version appearing in vol. II of the Schlechta edition.

8. See Plato, *The Republic*, especially 375a–375c, 411a–411e, and 439e–441c. The edition translated by Allan Bloom (New York: Basic Books, 1968) contains helpful material on thymos.

9. For suggestive references to *Armut*, see Schlechta, op. cit., vol. II, pp. 321, 363, 423, 521.

10. Ibid., p. 288.

11. In this essay I take the liberty of using Nietzsche and Zarathustra almost interchangeably. Nietzsche himself almost grants that liberty in *Ecce Homo*. In particular see Schlechta, op. cit., vol. II, pp. 1115–16, 1128–40.

12. For typical comments on "the good and the just," see ibid., pp. 459, 1156.

13. The only historical personage to be mentioned in the book, apart from Zarathustra, is Jesus, ibid., p. 335.

14. Ibid., p. 283.

15. Ibid., p. 293.

16. Ibid., p. 312.

17. Ibid., p. 306. An English translation of the speech, from which the quotation is taken, can be found in *Thus Spoke Zarathustra*, translated by Walter Kaufmann (New York: Penguin Books, 1978), pp. 40–41.

18. On Zarathustra's growing solitude, see my *Nietzsche's View of Socrates* (Ithaca: Cornell University Press, 1974), pp. 241–69.

19. See the prologue to *Thus Spoke Zarathustra* in Schlechta, op. cit., pp. 277–91.

20. Ibid., pp. 417–22.

21. Ibid., pp. 443–61.

22. Ibid., p. 343.

23. See especially Zarathustra's address to the "preachers of equality" in "On the Tarantulas," ibid., pp. 356–59.

24. Ibid., p. 420.

25. Ibid., p. 396–99.

26. Ibid., pp. 372–75.

27. For the spirit of revenge, see for examples, ibid., pp. 357, 395; For the spirit of gravity, see for examples, pp. 305–07, 406–11.

28. Nietzsche made this point in his early essay "On the Use and Disadvantage of History for Life." See Schlechta, op. cit., vol. I, p. 345.

29. For characteristic references to *Schwermut*, see Schlechta, op. cit., vol. II, pp. 310, 335, 405, 468–69, 501.

30. See especially ibid., p. 401.

31. Ibid., p. 433.

32. Ibid., pp. 407–08. I have used the translation by Walter Kaufmann, op. cit., p. 157.

33. See the beginning of *Beyond Good and Evil* in Schlechta, op. cit., vol. II, p. 565.

34. See ibid, pp. 328–30.

35. See especially the prologue, ibid., pp. 277–91.

36. Ibid., p. 294.

37. Ibid., pp. 413, 416, 423–24.

38. Ibid., p. 471.

39. Ibid., pp. 512–15.

40. Ibid., pp. 531–36.

41. Ibid., pp. 1240–42.

42. Ibid., p. 534.

43. Ibid., p. 524.

Index